MODERN HUMANITIES RESEARCH ASSOCIATION
NEW TRANSLATIONS
VOLUME 19

MICHEL-JEAN SEDAINE
LE PHILOSOPHE SANS LE SAVOIR

MODERN HUMANITIES RESEARCH ASSOCIATION
NEW TRANSLATIONS

The guiding principle of this series is to publish new translations into English of important works that have been hitherto imperfectly translated or that are entirely untranslated. The work to be translated or re-translated should be aesthetically or intellectually important. The proposal should cover such issues as copyright and, where relevant, an account of the faults of the previous translation/s; it should be accompanied by independent statements from two experts in the field attesting to the significance of the original work (in cases where this is not obvious) and to the desirability of a new or renewed translation.

Translations should be accompanied by a fairly substantial introduction and other, briefer, apparatus: a note on the translation; a select bibliography; a chronology of the author's life and works; and notes to the text.

Titles will be selected by members of the Editorial Board and edited by leading academics.

General Editor
Dr Ann Lewis

Editorial Board
Dr Ann Lewis (French)
Professor Ritchie Robertson (Germanic)
Professor Helena Sanson (Italian)
Professor David Gillespie (Slavonic)
Professor Duncan Wheeler (Spanish)
Professor Jonathan Thacker (Spanish)

www.translations.mhra.org.uk

Michel-Jean Sedaine
Le Philosophe sans le savoir

Translated by
Derek Connon

Modern Humanities Research Association
New Translations 19
2023

Published by

The Modern Humanities Research Association,
Salisbury House
Station Road
Cambridge CB1 2LA
United Kingdom

© Modern Humanities Research Association, 2023

Derek Connon has asserted his right under the Copyright, Designs and Patents Act 1988 to be identified as the author of this work. Parts of this work may be reproduced as permitted under legal provisions for fair dealing (or fair use) for the purposes of research, private study, criticism, or review, or when a relevant collective licensing agreement is in place. All other reproduction requires the written permission of the copyright holder who may be contacted at rights@mhra.org.uk.

First published 2023

ISBN 978-1-83954-543-6

For Tina

CONTENTS

Acknowledgements — viii
Introduction — 1
Le Philosophe sans le savoir — 19
Appendix of Revised Scenes — 97
Select Bibliography — 114

ACKNOWLEDGEMENTS

My thanks to Ann Lewis, without whom this translation would not have happened, and to Carolyn and Benjamin for being there.

INTRODUCTION

The first obstacle for the would-be translator of *Le Philosophe sans le savoir* arrives fairly quickly, for it is the title. It is true that there are those who simply get it wrong,[1] but amongst possible correct translations, if *The Philosopher Who Doesn't Know It* is lumpish and *The Unconscious Philosopher* has a potentially comic double meaning, *The Unintentional Philosopher*, *The Accidental Philosopher*, and *The Unwitting Philosopher* might all seem superficially acceptable. However, the word that might seem the most straightforward, *philosophe*, brings with it its own problems.

One of the most significant aspects of the intellectual and literary scene in eighteenth-century France was the existence of a group of artists and thinkers who challenged conventional attitudes and ideas. The range of their interests was vast, and, alongside issues that we might think of as conventionally belonging to the realms of philosophy, such as justice, religion, social equality, and education, they also wrote about science and medicine, mathematics, music, art, and literature. They were literary innovators, presenting their ideas in a variety of forms: letters, dialogues, novels, plays, and, moreover, they were adept at experimenting with those forms. They were far from being a unified group, but their shared aims and ideas gave them a certain solidarity, and one of the greatest products of the period, the twenty-eight volume *Encyclopédie*, begun under the editorship of Denis Diderot and Jean Le Rond d'Alembert and completed by Diderot alone, brought together articles by a huge range of like-minded authors.[2] It is to them that the title of Sedaine's play refers, and not only were they known as the *philosophes* to their contemporaries, when discussing them, even in English

---

[1] The version *The Philosopher without Knowledge* found in, amongst other places, the *Encyclopedia Britannica* (see https://www.britannica.com/biography/Michel-Jean-Sedaine [accessed 9 May 2022]), derives from a failure to take account of a basic principal of French grammar. The word *le* is both the masculine singular form of the definite article and the masculine singular form of the object pronoun (also used for genderless concepts), which precedes the verb; *savoir* is both a noun meaning 'knowledge' and the infinitive of the verb 'to know'. However, after the preposition *sans*, the definite article is not used before an unqualified noun, so the combination we have here must be pronoun plus infinitive. So, in order to mean *The Philosopher without Knowledge*, the title would have to be not *Le Philosophe sans le savoir*, but *Le Philosophe sans savoir*, although it is difficult to imagine any author choosing this form of words rather than the more idiomatic *Le Philosophe sans connaissances*.

[2] Although limited in some respects and very much of its time, Peter Gay's account of the *philosophes* still provides a useful overview (see his introduction to the two-volume *The Enlightenment: An Interpretation*: 'The Little Flock of *Philosophes*' (vol. I: *The Rise of Modern Paganism*, 3–19)).

contexts, the word tends still to be left in French. To combine an English and a French word as the two main words in a three-word title seems sufficiently uncomfortable for me to have decided that, rather like *Les Liaisons dangereuses* (pace the Hollywood film industry), *Così fan tutte*, and *La traviata*, it is a title better left untranslated.

There is, in fact, a tradition, originating with contemporaries of Sedaine, that the play initially had a different title, *Le Duel* (*The Duel*), even that this was Sedaine's own chosen title. Convenient as this title would be for the translator, Ira Owen Wade showed in a landmark article published in 1928 that the alternative title had nothing to do with Sedaine,[3] but that has not prevented the tale being repeated since then. Nevertheless, it is unlikely that, with that title, the play would have been as influential as it was with Sedaine's contemporaries or have retained its historical importance. For the actual title, which includes the only use of the word *philosophe* in the whole of the definitive version of the text, is the only concrete indication that the work is a contribution to a particular literary quarrel.

As is the way of things, if there was a group of eighteenth-century French writers known as the *philosophes*, there was bound to be a group of anti-*philosophes*, and it was one of them, Charles Palissot de Montenoy, who wrote a satirical comedy first performed on 2 May 1760 entitled *Les Philosophes* (*The Philosophes*).[4] In truth it is not a very good play. It owes a clear debt to Molière's comedy *Les Femmes savantes* (*The Learned Ladies*), amongst other sources, and commits a sin that Molière also committed in his play, but which tended to be avoided in satirical works at this time, which was to target not just a group of people, but specific individuals. The name of the character Dortidius, almost an anagram of his name with a Latinate suffix, made clear that a satire of Diderot was intended, and a vicious satire it was too; Claude Adrien Helvétius and Charles Pinot Duclos were also targeted, and whilst Jean-Jacques Rousseau otherwise gets off reasonably lightly, in one of the most notorious scenes in the play his philosophical focus on the state of nature is parodied when a character enters on all fours and, as a note in the text tells us, eats a lettuce. The play was something of a *succès de scandale*, clocking up fourteen performances in its initial run, although it then disappeared from the Parisian stage for more than twenty years.[5]

---

[3] See 'The Title of Sedaine's *Le Philosophe sans le savoir*'.
[4] For a recent translation of this play, see Charles Palissot, *The Philosophes*, translated by Jessica Goodman and others and edited by Jessica Goodman and Olivier Ferret, which also has a useful introduction by Goodman and Ferret. Hilde H. Freud, *Palissot and 'Les Philosophes'* is another useful source of information on Palissot and his play.
[5] A toned-down version of the play was revived by the Comédie-Française as a homage to the author along with three other plays of his between 1782 and 1784, when it received eleven performances; this coincided with a new edition of the text. (Statistics from the *Registres de la Comédie-Française* (*Registers of the Comédie-Française*) [accessed 10 May 2022]).

Voltaire is apparently not targeted; he was such an influential figure that Palissot presumably did not want to make an enemy of him, and, in the letter published as a preface to the printed edition, albeit without naming him, he even resorts to flattery in a denial that there is any criticism of him in the play. However, this did not prevent Voltaire from coming to the defence of his fellows. He first wrote a series of letters to Palissot urging a retraction of the play, then, when Palissot responded by publishing the letters, in September 1760 republished the author's prefatory letter with his own critical commentary in an anonymous collection entitled *Recueil de facéties parisiennes* (*Collection of Parisian Pleasantries*). Before that, on 26 July 1760, he had allowed the Comédie-Française to give the first performance of his *Le Café; ou, l'Écossaise* (*The Café; or, The Scottish Girl*). Unfortunately, whilst the play was very successful,[6] its effectiveness as a riposte to Palissot's work is somewhat compromised by the fact that it had clearly not been written as a specific response (it had already been published in May), and so, although it attacks the anti-*philosophe* faction, it does not specifically target Palissot, but directs its criticism against another of the anti-*philosophes* and one of his supporters, Élie Fréron, author of the periodical *L'Année littéraire* (*The Literary Year*), who is transparently the source of the character Frélon, a name which is clearly a cross between Fréron and the French word for a hornet, *frelon*. So, despite its success, there was perhaps still room for a more specific reply to Palissot.

Michel-Jean Sedaine writes of how he came to intervene in a text entitled 'Quelques réflexions inédites de Sedaine sur l'opéra comique' ('Some Unpublished Thoughts of Sedaine on *Opéra-Comique*'), published by René-Charles Guilbert de Pixerécourt in the fourth volume of his *Théâtre choisi* (*Selected Plays*):

> In 1765 [*sic*], finding myself at the first performance of *Les Philosophes* (a mediocre and malicious work in three acts), I was outraged at the way that honest men of letters whom I knew only by their works were treated. To reconcile the public with the idea of the word *philosophe*, which this satire risked damaging, I wrote *Le Philosophe sans le savoir*.[7]

---

[6] It received twenty-one performances in its first season, and was performed 132 times at the Comédie-Française between 1760 and 1793 (*Registres de la Comédie-Française* [accessed 12 May 2022]). We should note that, although this database allows us to form an accurate impression of the contemporary success of these plays in Paris, it ends at the 1792–1793 season. We need to bear in mind both that successful works like *Le Philosophe sans le savoir* would have received a significant number of performances in the provinces or even abroad (see below for details of translations), and that, after the disruption caused by the Revolution, although some works lost their foothold in the repertoire, successful plays continued to be performed in the nineteenth century and often beyond.

[7] 'Quelques réflexions inédites de Sedaine sur l'opéra comique', p. 509. All translations in this introduction are my own. This is a rather odd location to find such a text. Pixerécourt explains in a footnote that the manuscript was given to him in gratitude after Sedaine's death by one of

Up until 1760 Sedaine had concentrated mainly on writing the text for *opéras-comiques*,[8] and this would continue to be his principal activity, which may explain why it took him so long to write his response to Palissot, which was not performed until 1765 (which presumably explains the slip in the quotation above), although at least some of that time was taken up with struggles to persuade the censors to allow it to be performed. Paradoxically, given the constant problems that the *philosophes* had with the censors, their reservations apparently had nothing to do with the philosophical content of the play, but derived from the fact that the plot centred on a duel, duelling being illegal:

> Never has a work found it as difficult as this one to be staged: it took me a whole year to get permission. They said that the title of the play was *The Duel*, and that it was an apologia for duelling. The prejudices against the work were so strong that I would never have obtained permission to have it staged if the Lieutenant de Police and the Procureur du Roi had not come to a rehearsal given to allow them to hear the work so they could make a judgment. Permission was at last granted.[9]

One result of this struggle was that Sedaine was forced to adapt his text, mainly by cutting any passages that seemed too tolerant of the practice of duelling, but also by strengthening the justification of the laws banning it. The published edition corresponded with the version performed, but Sedaine did manage to get round the law to an extent, by producing a separately paginated supplement containing the original versions of passages cut or adapted that was inserted into some copies either in the body of the text, or at the end as an appendix.[10]

Still, the result was clearly worth the time and the struggle, for it was a huge success, outdoing both *Les Philosophes* and *L'Écossaise* in its first season with

---

his daughters for whom Pixerécourt had arranged a pension from the Opéra-Comique, and that he wishes to make it available to the public. Whilst there seems to be no reason to disbelieve this account, the fact that the manuscript appears to have disappeared means that we cannot confirm it. We should also note that Sedaine was a friend of Diderot, so, in his case at least, the claim that he did not know the *philosophes* except by their works is not true.

[8] *Opéra-comique* is the French term for opera with spoken dialogue between numbers. Originating at the Parisian Fairs, it originally made use of pre-existing tunes, but, by the time Sedaine was working on it, the music was specially composed. Sedaine was also one of the authors who began to introduce more serious subjects into what had originally been an exclusively comic genre. (See below on the significance of the word *comique* in this context.) Sedaine collaborated with a number of composers, most frequently François-André Philidor, Pierre-Alexandre Monsigny, and André Grétry.

[9] 'Quelques réflexions inédites de Sedaine sur l'opéra comique', pp. 509-10. See in the introduction to his edition of the play (pp. 24-47) John Dunkley's detailed discussion of legislation relating to duelling and its importance for *Le Philosophe sans le savoir*. Dunkley's excellent introduction is a mine of information on issues relevant to the play, but, being in French, will not be accessible to all readers of this translation.

[10] For more information on this and details about how it is handled in the present translation, see below.

twenty-eight performances, and receiving a total of 107 performances at the Comédie-Française between 1765 and 1793.[11] And its success continued; George Sand staged a sequel, *Le Mariage de Victorine* (*The Marriage of Victorine*), in 1851, and a version made for television was broadcast in 1966,[12] a remarkable event when we consider that, from the entire repertoire of French eighteenth-century drama, it is only really the major works of Marivaux and two plays from Beaumarchais's Figaro trilogy that have generally survived on the stage into the twentieth and twenty-first centuries.[13]

So how does Sedaine set about rehabilitating the word *philosophe*, and in what sense is Vanderk *père* our unwitting *philosophe*? The character we are presented with is an overwhelmingly good man. He believes everyone to be deserving of respect, for human worth is not dependent on social rank; hence, even a servant should not be kept waiting, and the realization that Desparville *père* is the father of his son's opponent in the duel does not change his attitude to him. He is also a fair dealer in business: he does not exploit his customers, and he instils notions of truth and honesty in his children too. He is indulgent of human folly, as we see particularly through the figure of the aunt, but also by his calm acceptance of the mistake made by his son. He also, in a passage that was cut in the performing version of the play, shows religious tolerance: the fact that the colour of the ribbon on Desparville *père*'s medal reveals him to be a Protestant does not cause him to treat him differently.[14] He respects the law, but this does not prevent him from questioning it: he understands why the laws against duelling are as they are, but questions their effectiveness. And he is stoical in the face of a situation that he cannot change. These are all traits that we will find in the writings of the *philosophes*. And as well as rehabilitating the figure of the *philosophe*, the play also seeks to rehabilitate the figure of the merchant, who had traditionally been, in both drama and the novel, an unscrupulous villain. So Vanderk *père* is a paragon of honesty, and his great speech suggesting that the trade of the merchant is more important than monarchs and war, keeping society working despite them, is one of the most eloquent, even poetic passages in the play.

---

[11] See *Registres de la Comédie-Française* [accessed 12 May 2022].
[12] Broadcast on ORTF 2 on 27 August 1966 at 9.00pm, it was directed by Jean-Paul Roux.
[13] Further evidence of the play's success is found in the large number of published editions and the existence of translations, of which I have found five: two anonymous translations into German with the title *Der Philosoph ohne es zu wissen* published in 1767 and 1776, a version in English entitled *The Duel*, translated by William O'Brien and published in 1772, a Danish version entitled *Den virkelig Viise*, translated by Frederik Schwarz, and one translated into Italian as *Il filosofo senza saper d'esserlo* by Placido Bordoni published in 1805. O'Brien's English version, although interesting, is relatively free; I have not made use of it in my own translation.
[14] Some of the *philosophes* were atheists or Deists, some were not, but they generally shared a disapproval of the prejudice and cruelty brought about by organized religion. Since this cut bears no relation to the theme of the duel, it may provide us with one piece of evidence that the censors were also anxious about any 'philosophical' content in the play.

And yet, Sedaine's play does not entirely escape literary tradition, and there are times when that literary tradition seems to work against the message he seeks to convey. Perhaps most obvious, in a play that aims to question the prejudices associated with social rank and promotes the idea of individual merit, is the fact that our humble merchant should turn out not to be humble at all, but to be an aristocrat. This does allow Sedaine to depict a character who, despite his nobility, sees no shame in embracing a characteristically bourgeois lifestyle by pursuing a trade, thus promoting the importance of the bourgeoisie for the functioning of society. It also allows him to satirize false ideas of nobility via Vanderk *père*'s ridiculous sister, a female version of the comically pretentious *marquis* found in some of Molière's comedies. But it certainly undermines the depiction of social mobility initially suggested by the fact that the daughter of a member of the bourgeoisie is able to marry a Président, because we quickly find out that he is not a member of the bourgeoisie at all.[15] This also has implications for Sedaine's efforts to rehabilitate the figure of the merchant. As we have noted, traditionally merchants, financiers, and money lenders had been depicted in literature, whether plays or novels, as dishonest, out to exploit their customers; Lesage's comedy *Turcaret* provides us with perhaps the most famous example in eighteenth-century French literature, but it is far from being the only one. In Vanderk *père* Sedaine provides us with a clear contradiction of this generalization, but, problematically, he is not only an exception in the field of French literature, he is also an exception within Sedaine's play itself, for Desparville *père* tells us of encounters with other financiers, all of whom confirm the general stereotype. It is true that Vanderk *père* is a merchant whose business would have embraced a wide range of activities and not, like the others, a professional money lender, but we are still potentially left with a feeling of unease, because not only does a single exception provide a somewhat unconvincing refutation of the stereotype, it also leaves us with the impression that Sedaine may be suggesting that it is Vanderk *père*'s very nobility which makes him into an exception, for, although literature is of course not free of aristocratic villains, it is nevertheless true that in other literary contexts nobility often provides proof of a character's superiority.[16]

---

[15] The idea of the rise of the bourgeoisie at this period features in much academic writing, and the drama of the period does seem to promote self-consciously the values associated with the merchant class, however, it is not universally accepted; see, for instance, Sarah Maza, *The Myth of the French Bourgeoisie: An Essay on the Social Imaginary, 1750–1850*.

[16] In the introduction to his edition John Dunkley discusses in detail the activities of the merchant and also the complex relationship between the successful members of the merchant class and the nobility (see in particular pp. 12–19), and an invaluable English-language source on this aspect of the play is H. T. Mason, '*Le Philosophe sans le savoir*: An Aristocratic *Drame Bourgeois*?'. In 1767 legislation was passed allowing a nobleman to operate as a merchant without forfeiting his noble rank, but in 1765 it is the fact that he practises maritime commerce that allows Vanderk to retain his title.

INTRODUCTION

There is also in the play a clear and surprising class division. The ridiculing of the aunt's snobbery might suggest to us that Sedaine is generally critical of class distinction, but this is not strictly true. Yes, Vanderk *père* may criticize Antoine for keeping a servant waiting on the grounds that his time may be precious, but the reason his time may be precious is because his master may need him, not because of any inconvenience caused to the servant himself. The relationship between Vanderk *père* and Antoine is interesting in its own right. They have been friends since Vanderk's self-exile after his involvement in a duel; they were companions in arms when the ship of Vanderk's Dutch benefactor was attacked, and yet, the fact that they are master and servant, nobleman and commoner, is always present: Antoine is the very model of the faithful old retainer and not his master's social equal. Similarly, Victorine clearly has a strong affection for Vanderk *fils*, and he is obviously sympathetically disposed to her, but any suggestion of a romantic involvement that could lead to marriage is entirely one-sided. George Sand may well have Victorine marry the young Vanderke (as she spells it) in her sequel *Le Mariage de Victorine* and argue in her preface that she believes that this would have been Sedaine's intention had he written a sequel,[17] in eighteenth-century theatre love across the social divide will always be resolved by a recognition scene in which it is discovered that the character thought to be a social inferior is, in fact, an equal. Sedaine's back story of the relationship between Vanderk *père* and Antoine is detailed enough to make it clear that there is no possibility of that happening in either this play or a sequel, but neither is there any suggestion that Vanderk *père*, who has, after all, just married his daughter to a Président, regards Victorine as a future daughter-in-law, or indeed, that Vanderk *fils* sees her as a future wife. Moreover, the fact that Victorine's mother was wet nurse to Vanderk *fils*, as we discover in the very first scene of the play, whilst traditionally in French culture suggesting a special bond between them, they are *frère* and *sœur de lait* ('milk brother and sister'), also underlines the breadth of the social divide between them: people from families that employ wet nurses do not marry people from the families of women who perform this service.

One defining characteristic of Sedaine's play is his frequent use of comedy in a work which, despite the generic description *comédie* on its title page, has at its centre an issue of genuine seriousness, and Sedaine casts his net wide in his reworking of comic traditions. We have noted that the comic figure of Vanderk *père*'s sister the Marquise follows in the tradition of Molière's mockery of the pretentions of the minor nobility in his *marquis* characters. Another tradition that he calls on is comedy arising from the guilelessness of the young, which is found both in the naïvety of the scene in which Sophie Vanderk is announced to

---

[17] *Le Mariage de Victorine, pour faire suite au 'Philosophe sans le savoir' de Sedaine* (*The Marriage of Victorine, to Act as a Sequel to Sedaine's 'Philosophe sans le savoir'*), pp. 5–6.

her father as Madame de Vanderville and in the character of Victorine.[18] However, another tradition in comedy is that the roles of lower-class or servant characters tend to feature broader comedy than those of the masters, and in *Le Philosophe sans le savoir*, in which the central plotline is not comic at all, this tradition is clearly reflected in the fact that the roles of the principal upper-class characters – the male Vanderks and the Desparvilles – remain serious, whilst the servants, Antoine, Victorine, the servant who falls asleep while waiting to see Vanderk *père*, and the group of musicians, all have more or less comic roles. So, we take the characters who are social inferiors less seriously than we do the members of the nobility, which has a tendency to back up this sense of an ingrained hierarchy that is particularly surprising in the case of Antoine, given his important involvement in the events surrounding the duel.

The mention of the fact that *Le Philosophe sans le savoir* bears on its title page the generic designation *comédie* when it is not predominantly comic brings us to the question of exactly what sort of play it is.

One feature of eighteenth-century French drama was an increasing taste for sentimentality. It can be found in tragedies like Antoine Houdar de La Motte's *Inès de Castro* (1723) or Voltaire's *Zaïre* (1732), but it was in comedy that it became most famous, with Pierre-Claude Nivelle de La Chaussée developing the genre that became known as *comédie larmoyante* (tearful comedy). The ratio of the comic to the sentimental in La Chaussée's works varied: *La Fausse Antipathie* (*The False Antipathy*) (1733) and *Le Préjugé à la mode* (*The Fashionable Prejudice*) (1735) are genuinely comic, but one of the most famous, *Mélanide* (1741) is almost entirely serious. Voltaire was not the only one to pick up on the genre, although he, having objected to the term *comédie larmoyante*, had to invent another way of describing his own works of this type, calling them *comédies attendrissantes* (touching comedies); *L'Écossaise* is one of these, alongside *L'Enfant prodigue* (*The Prodigal Son*) (1736) and *Nanine* (1749).

The notion that theatre should have an educational value had always been around; the formula 'plaire et instruire' ('please and instruct') was seen as a basic tenet, but there was an increased didacticism in eighteenth-century theatre. Tragedies began to have philosophical points to make, and, whilst seventeenth-century authors of comedy took the view that people belonged to certain character types and would not change, so that dénouements found happy endings by circumventing the central character's personality flaw, in eighteenth-century comedy the central characters began to see the light and reform at the end of the play.

---

[18] Again, this can be found in Molière, although in perhaps the best example, the scene between the central character Argan and his little daughter Louison in *Le Malade imaginaire* (*The Imaginary Invalid*) (II. 8), the child is much younger than either Sophie or Victorine.

Meanwhile, in England, the form known as domestic tragedy was developing: these plays placed ordinary people in situations which tried their moral worth and found them wanting, leading to the tragic ending which reinforced the moral lesson. Diderot particularly admired Aaron Hill's *The Fatal Extravagance* (1721), George Lillo's *The London Merchant* (1731), and Edward Moore's *The Gamester* (1753), and would go on to make his own translation of the last of these in 1760 and even to seek, unsuccessfully, to have it performed on the French stage.

Following on from these trends, Diderot set out to create a new theatrical form.[19] Traditional tragedy dealt exclusively with mythical or historical figures, which meant that contemporary people featured only in comedy, where they were generally treated as figures of fun. What Diderot sought was a new theatrical genre in which members of his own class, the bourgeoisie, could be treated seriously. In this way, he felt, people could learn about their own social and moral responsibilities via plays which touched their emotions. Hence, rather than mocking ridiculous character traits, in the way that traditional comedy had done, the new drama would show positive images of different social roles by taking as its focus social condition. He began his campaign to create this new genre with two plays, each accompanied by a theoretical work: *Le Fils naturel* (*The Natural Son*), which was followed by a series of dialogues which are generally known as the *Entretiens sur 'Le Fils naturel'* (*Conversations on 'The Natural Son'*) (1757), and *Le Père de famille* (*The Father of a Family*), which was accompanied by an essay entitled *De la poésie dramatique* (*On Dramatic Poetry*) (1758). Rather oddly for someone attempting to launch a theatrical revolution, Diderot did not really intend the first of these for performance; rather the play was to be read as part of the 'sort of novel' that he said it formed with the accompanying *Entretiens*, and, when he did eventually get around to having it performed at the Comédie-Française in 1771, it was a failure, receiving only a single performance. *Le Père de famille*, on the other hand, was relatively successful, receiving twenty performances in its first two seasons at the Comédie-Française, and totalling 123 performances at that same theatre up until 1793.[20]

The theory set out in the two theoretical works calls for a theatre which makes a direct appeal to the audience by being as realistic as possible: hence Diderot advocated the use of prose rather than verse, realistic sets and costumes, and, whilst comedy was not banned, the overall aim was to take the characters and their predicaments seriously. In the event, though, whilst *Le Fils naturel* is entirely serious, *Le Père de famille*, like *Le Philosophe sans le savoir*, does have comic elements, and one of the reasons for the success of Sedaine's play is surely that it contains more comic elements than the majority of plays in the genre.

---

[19] See on the subject of Diderot and the theatre Derek Connon, *Innovation and Renewal: A Study of the Theatrical Works of Diderot*.
[20] *Registres de la Comédie-Française* [accessed 18 May 2022].

Diderot was also interested in the creation of a more natural type of dialogue. He pointed out that the tendency in traditional theatre for characters in the grip of emotion to deliver long poetic speeches was illogical: extreme emotion makes individuals less, not more eloquent, and theatrical dialogue should reflect this.[21] Sedaine made a similar point in the speech he made on the occasion of his entry into the Académie Française:

> The theatre, whether tragic or comic, is fuelled by emotions, and sometimes their force dares to break the strict rules of grammatical correctness. It is true that these transgressions must be required by the passion of the personalities, by the force of the situation, or by the speed of the action, and that they should result in moments of beauty.[22]

This led, in the case of both authors, to much use of unfinished phrases ending in ellipses, exclamatory syllables and remarks, and rhetorical questions. However, in addition to a new approach to the verbal aspect of theatre, Diderot also sought to develop the visual, advocating the use of gesture and suggesting that the surprise produced by *coups de théâtre* should be replaced by points of repose where the placement of the actors formed touching tableaux worthy of the painter's art.

In the *Entretiens sur 'Le Fils naturel'*, one of the characters, when asked to give a name to this new dramatic genre, suggests 'la tragédie domestique et bourgeoise' ('domestic and bourgeois tragedy'),[23] but most plays in the genre having happy endings, in the event it came to be known as *drame* or *drame bourgeois*. The term *drame* is simply the French word for 'drama', but, rather like *philosophe*, in English contexts it tends to be kept in French when referring to this specific genre. We should, however, be careful about the use of the term 'bourgeois'. Despite Diderot's use of it in relation to tragedy in the *Entretiens*, the term *drame bourgeois* is not his, and his two plays in the form were, like *Le Philosophe sans le savoir*, originally designated simply with the word *comédie*, and whilst the three principal male characters in *Le Fils naturel* bear the sort of unrealistic names characteristic of French classical comedy, Dorval, Clairville, and Lysimond, it is clear that they live a life unencumbered by the need to follow a profession, and the two adult male characters in *Le Père de famille*, Monsieur d'Orbesson and his brother-in-law the Commandeur d'Auvillé have, in the case of the first, the nobiliary particle and, in the case of the second, a title that designate them as members of the nobility. Diderot's desire to write drama about ordinary people clearly did not exclude the minor nobility, and, that being the case, Vanderk's nobility is not, perhaps, as surprising as the subsequent use of the term *drame bourgeois* might make it seem.

---

[21] See *Entretiens sur 'Le Fils naturel'*, pp. 101–02.
[22] *Discours prononcés dans l'Académie Françoise*, p. 6.
[23] *Entretiens sur 'Le Fils naturel'*, p. 119.

So why, then, do the title pages of *Le Philosophe sans le savoir* and Diderot's two *drames* bear the generic description *comédie*? This is, in fact, typical of almost all the *drames*, in their early editions at least. The term *drame* had not been established, leaving to authors only the choice of *comédie* and *tragédie*, and the latter not only implied a death or deaths at the end, it was also in the French theatre closely associated with plays dealing with characters from classical mythology or history.[24] So this left *comédie*. But we should be aware that the term is not a straightforward equivalent of the English 'comedy'. Whilst most plays written before the *drames* that were designated as *comédies* were, or were at least intended to be, funny, other uses of the term and its derivatives are more ambiguous. The standard term in French for any actor is 'un comédien'; the Comédie-Française is the French national theatre, and performs drama of all sorts, including tragedy; and, although early examples of the form invariably were comic, the second part of the term *opéra-comique* refers not to that, but to the presence of spoken dialogue between the musical numbers – hence the fact that Sedaine and others could begin introducing more serious elements into their *opéras-comiques*, and that Bizet's *Carmen* can be an *opéra-comique* despite ending with the death of its female protagonist. Consequently, the term *comédie* was not as inappropriate, even for those *drames* with no comic elements, as it might at first appear to the anglophone reader.

Diderot attracted some significant disciples, and one of these was his friend Sedaine himself, who, in addition to *Le Philosophe sans le savoir*, wrote another successful, albeit predominantly comic, work in the genre, *La Gageure imprévue* (*The Unexpected Wager*) (1768), as well as introducing elements of the new genre into some of his *opéras-comiques*. Pierre-Augustin Caron de Beaumarchais, the only French playwright from the second half of the eighteenth-century still to be performed regularly on the modern stage, was another follower, his first two major works for the stage both being *drames*: *Eugénie* (1767) and *Les Deux Amis* (*The Two Friends*) (1770).[25] If he then moved away from the genre to write the first two plays in his Figaro trilogy,[26] he returned to it for the third, *La Mère coupable* (*The Guilty Mother*) (1791).

---

[24] There are a small number of examples of *drames* designated *tragédies*. For instance, Bernard-Joseph Saurin described his *Béverlei* as a *tragédie bourgeoise*; on the one hand this is clearly justified by the death of the central character at the end, but the fact that Saurin chose to write in verse, rather than the prose suggested by Diderot, may derive from the feeling that he needed to live up to the tragic genre. More unusually, Diderot himself also used the term for a now largely forgotten one-act play designed for domestic performance called *Les Pères malheureux* (*The Unhappy Fathers*) which, although predominantly touching and sentimental, does have a happy ending.

[25] The latter follows on from *Le Philosophe sans le savoir* in presenting a sympathetic portrait of a merchant.

[26] It is, of course, these two plays, *Le Barbier de Séville* (*The Barber of Seville*) (1775) and *Le Mariage de Figaro* (*The Marriage of Figaro*) (1784), which retain their place on the

Diderot recognized the quality of *Le Philosophe sans le savoir* immediately, and his enthusiasm knew no bounds. In a letter to his friend Friedrich Melchior Grimm written the day after the first performance, which Grimm published in the issue for 15 December 1765 of his *Correspondance littéraire* (*Literary Correspondence*),[27] Diderot recounts saying to the engraver Charles-Nicolas Cochin:

> I feel keenly the full extent of the merit of this work. I'll state it as loudly and as truthfully as possible; and there is no one to whom it should do more harm than to me, because this man has beaten me to it.[28]

He also recalled his enthusiasm later when he wrote his *Paradoxe sur le comédien* (*Paradox of the Actor*):

> *Le Philosophe sans le savoir* had a rocky reception at its first and second performances, and I was very upset; at the third, it was praised to the skies, and I was beside myself with happiness. The following morning, I threw myself into a fiacre, and I rushed off in search of Sedaine. It was winter, and it was most bitterly cold. I went everywhere that I hoped I might find him. I discovered that he was deep in the Faubourg Saint-Antoine, and I had myself taken there. I went up to him; I threw my arms around his neck; I could hardly speak, and tears were running down my cheeks.[29]

The genre initially enjoyed a distinct success, and was also highly influential. As well as influencing the development of *opéra-comique* in the second part of the eighteenth century in the way that we have noted, it was exported to Germany by Gotthold Ephraim Lessing where it reverted to the tragic mood of its English forebears as *bürgerliches Trauerspiel* (bourgeois tragedy) and was also taken up by Friedrich Schiller. Back in France, its high emotionalism developed into the sensationalistic *mélodrame*, as practised in early nineteenth-century Paris by authors such as Guilbert de Pixerécourt, Victor Ducange, and Adolphe d'Ennery;

---

contemporary stage and keep his reputation alive, even if, outside of the French-speaking world, this is largely thanks to the operas by Rossini and Mozart.

[27] Grimm's, *Correspondance littéraire, philosophique et critique* (*Literary, Philosophical, and Critical Correspondence*) was a literary newsletter sent in manuscript copies twice a month to its small group of subscribers, all powerful aristocrats living outside of France. As well as Grimm's own commentaries on life in Paris, it included works by other authors, including some of Diderot's most important texts.

[28] *Correspondance littéraire*, VI, 442.

[29] *Paradoxe sur le comédien*, p. 330. Because of numerous revisions, this work is difficult to date, but it seems to have reached its final form in 1777 or '78. A further oft-repeated anecdote says that after a reading of the work before it was performed an enthusiastic Diderot said to Sedaine: 'My friend, if you weren't so old, I would give you my daughter', but as this appears for the first time with no indication of its source in an editor's note to an edition of the *Correspondance littéraire* edited by Jules-Antoine Taschereau and published in 1829, its authenticity cannot be guaranteed (see *Correspondance littéraire*, VI, 441).

melodrama would also become popular in Victorian Britain.[30] The influence of the genre can also be felt in those nineteenth-century plays that bore the title *drame* by authors such as Eugène Scribe, Alexandre Dumas *fils*, and Émile Augier. But the combination of didacticism, high emotion, and sentimentality that characterizes most *drames* meant that it was a genre that was very much of its time, and was unlikely to last in its original form; in his late and sadly neglected comedy *Est-il bon? Est-il méchant?* (*Is He Good? Is He Wicked?*) (1784), not only has Diderot abandoned the genre himself, but he has the central character, who is clearly a self-portrait, comment on having been to the reading of 'an appalling *drame*, as they all are'.[31]

Nevertheless, in terms of critical opinion, *Le Philosophe sans le savoir* holds a special place. Félix Gaiffe, in his monumental study *Le Drame en France au XVIIIe siècle* (*The 'Drame' in France in the Eighteenth Century*), published in 1910, took the view that its high quality made it a unique exception in the history of the *drame*,[32] and, although many neglected genres have been revived and rehabilitated since then, the *drame* has conspicuously not been one of them. So what is it that makes *Le Philosophe sans le savoir* so exceptional?

First of all, there is the plot, which combines the depiction of a happy family occasion with something much darker. The dramatic effect of the dilemma that this creates for Vanderk *père* and *fils*, as well as Antoine, is intensified by their need to keep the problem secret from the rest of the family. That in itself creates an interesting contrast between those who are in the know, and those who are not, with the confused and anxious Victorine somehow positioned between the two. The frame for the action is, of course, the marriage of Sophie Vanderk, the sort of happy family gathering that illustrates the ideal that should, in the terms of the didactic mission of the *drame*, be sought by us all, but against that is set the theme of the duel, an institution that destroys families, for the force of the law means that even the victor must flee the country and so abandon his family. And although it could be argued that, despite having gone through this experience himself, Vanderk *père* has managed to build himself a happy life, it is also true that his experience gives him a unique insight into the challenge faced by his son, and it is on the fate of Vanderk *fils* that our emotional investment is concentrated. The audience's response to this is intensified by a double *coup de théâtre* (despite

---

[30] Etymologically the term 'melodrama' refers to the combination of the spoken word with a musical accompaniment, and this is how it was exclusively used up until the end of the eighteenth century, and still is in some contexts. The *mélodrames* and melodramas of the nineteenth century were so called because they were characterized by significant use of background music to support the dramatic action. It is from them that the more common modern use of the word to describe theatre which is exaggeratedly dramatic and emotional derives.

[31] *Est-il bon? Est-il méchant?*, p. 64.

[32] See *Le Drame en France au XVIIIe siècle*, pp. 337–39, particularly p. 339.

Diderot's dislike of them), when first of all the three knocks on the door signal the death of the son, only for relief to come with his unexpected entry onto the stage, fit and well. The emotional intensity of the first of these is significantly increased by the fact that the three knocks occur while Vanderk *père* is engaged in business with Desparville *père* whom by now he knows to be the father of his son's adversary. The combination of his stoicism in continuing his business dealings and his generosity in refusing to take out his feelings on Desparville *père* of course provide evidence of his status as a *philosophe*. He is able to exercise reason despite the emotion of the situation, whereas Desparville *père* will prove himself less philosophical by his later admission that he would not have been able to overcome his emotional response in the same way (V. 11), and it is, of course, by allowing his emotions to take over instead of exercising reason that Vanderk *fils* brings about the duel in the first place. And lest we might think that the device of the three knocks is pushing the drama of the situation too far to be credible, Sedaine tells us in the document published by Pixerécourt that it was based on a real-life event which occurred while he was writing *Le Philosophe sans le savoir*:

> At that same time, a nobleman fought a duel on the road to Sèvres. His father was in his residence awaiting the news of the result of the encounter, and had given orders that, if his son was dead, all that should be done was to give three knocks on the porte cochère. That is what gave me the idea for the knocks I used in the play.[33]

Of course, we cannot be sure whether this is true or simply a way of justifying the most obviously theatrical event in the play (I know of no evidence either way), but it surely also carries a metaphorical message. There is already clear irony in Vanderk *père*'s suggestion earlier in the play that his son may be planning to stage a play on the wedding day, 'a tragedy perhaps' (act II. 4). The three knocks on the door, echoing the three knocks struck with the staff known as the *brigadier* that traditionally herald the beginning of a play in France, seem to be an indication that the tragedy has begun, although it will, of course, be averted.

The tone of the play is lightened by the use of comedy, and also by the deftness of the dialogue, which, although it conforms to both the taste for didacticism and the use of fragmentary writing characteristic of the *drame*, nevertheless has a lightness of touch not usually found in plays in the genre, only rarely descending into long (and they are never particularly long) moralizing speeches.

Still, whilst after a shaky first night or two, the play became popular with audiences, it had, as we have noted, struggled with the censors and police not because of its association with the *philosophes*, but because of the use of duelling as a subject.[34] It is true that plays such as Corneille's *Le Cid* and *Horace*, in which

---

[33] 'Quelques réflexions inédites de Sedaine sur l'opéra comique', p. 509.
[34] Although Ira Owen Wade suggests that the censors were merely using the issue of the duel

the heroes fight and win duels, formed part of the standard theatrical repertoire, but they both placed duelling in a historical context, one in medieval Spain, the other in the legendary early history of Rome. Sedaine's duel takes place in contemporary France, and this proved too much for the authorities. In an effort to curb the huge loss of life caused by duels over matters of honour, increasingly rigorous laws banning them had been introduced under Louis XIII and Louis XIV, but the practice continued to be a problem during the eighteenth century. Sedaine presents and discusses the problems with subtlety. Despite the illegality of the practice, there is no way out for the person challenged to a duel, or, indeed, in the case of Vanderk *fils*, for a challenger who changes his mind. To refuse a duel is to lose face, and consequently to gain a reputation for cowardice that will attract other aggressors. To participate in a duel was not only to risk being killed, but was also to suffer the full force of the law if one were the survivor, which could result in either confiscation of assets and loss of rank, or the threat of execution. Hence, in most cases, the survivor would take flight. So Vanderk *père* had his life changed by being forced to flee after his duel, and we see both him and Desparville *père* making plans to help their sons if they happen to be the survivor. Clearly, in doing this, both fathers are breaking the law, no matter how much Vanderk *père* speaks of the laws against duelling being justified. However, the play also gives evidence that, despite the rigour of these laws, they were not always rigorously applied: Vanderk *père* has returned to France, and, although he lives incognito under a false name, he has not forfeited his rank, and uses his title in the marriage contract. Vanderk *fils* and Desparville *fils* complete their duel, all that is needed for honour to be satisfied is for both to shoot, which they do, but, because no one is killed, they and their fathers clearly take the view that, legally at least, it is as if nothing has happened. After a long battle with the authorities, agreement was eventually given for certain passages to be rewritten to reduce the impact of this aspect of the plot before performance was allowed, although Grimm recounts an amusing anecdote about how Sedaine contrived to ensure that permission to perform the play was granted. When three of the magistrates responsible for making the decision about the play's future attended the rehearsal at the Comédie-Française mentioned above to make their judgment, Sedaine requested that they bring their wives with them. To protests that the women knew nothing about the legal aspects of the case, Sedaine replied that they could pass judgment on the rest. It appears that the magistrates were swayed by the fact that their wives wept throughout the performance.[35]

As we have already noted, Sedaine managed to include in the published edition of the work a separately paginated supplement giving the original text of the

---

to suppress a work that could inflame opposition between the *philosophes* and the anti-*philosophes*. See 'The Title of Sedaine's *Le Philosophe sans le savoir*', pp. 1032-33.
[35] See *Correspondance littéraire*, VI, 438-39.

scenes or part scenes which had to be modified, but, as he points out in his introduction to that supplement that it also includes passages that were changed as a result of audience response, we cannot be absolutely certain which changes were made to appease the censor and which were not. We can be certain of two that were not changed because of censorship, as they are mentioned in that introduction: clearly the comic interruption of the musicians at one of the tensest points in the work proved too much for audiences that were relatively unused to the mixing of the comic and the serious, and Vanderk *père*'s generosity in responding readily to Desparville *père*'s request to be paid in gold after he has heard the three knocks was clearly thought to be taking tolerance too far, and so the request was moved to earlier in the scene. But what of the suppression of the indications that the Desparvilles are Protestants? This is unrelated to the theme of duelling, so was it changed at the request of the censors, or not? And, if not, what was the motivation for the change? It is certainly a detail that adds significantly to the depiction of Vanderk *père* as an unwitting *philosophe*, but was it thought too daring to introduce the question of religion into a text where it is not otherwise a theme?

The reasons for other changes are clearer: references to the help Vanderk *père* is prepared to give his son are reduced or removed, and changes are not limited to cutting, as the speech in which Vanderk *père* defends the laws against duelling as just is significantly extended. Still, as we might suspect from the fact that Sedaine was anxious to include those original versions in the published text, he did not regard the revised version as anything other than a compromise, and he tells us in the introduction to the supplement that in countries that do not have the same moral attitudes or censorship rules as France, it is his original version that he wished to be performed.

The Text of the Translation

This brings us neatly to the question of which text of *Le Philosophe sans le savoir* to base a translation on. Rather than using the first edition of 1766, which has numerous errors, there is general agreement among editors of the French text that the corrected second edition, published in the same year, is to be preferred. These two editions are also the only ones published during Sedaine's lifetime to include the supplement containing the original text of those sections modified to appease the censors, and so I have followed them in basing my translation on that same second edition.

Next, as we have noted, Sedaine was forced to cut his text to satisfy the authorities before his play could be performed, and it is also that censored version that was published in his lifetime, although, as we have also seen, the published text also has cuts made by Sedaine in response to audience reaction to certain episodes. Should a translation reproduce the experience of the original readers and give the cut text accompanied by the supplement, or should it take note of Sedaine's wish and reconstruct the original text? Again, I have followed in the path of most editors of the French text, and have restored the sections included in the supplement to their original place in the work, so recreating Sedaine's original version. I have, however, adopted a different solution to other editors in the matter of what to do with those sections of the published text that have been replaced by the text of the supplement. One interesting feature of the supplement is how much of the text is identical to the equivalent sections of the main printed text. Had Sedaine chosen to reproduce in the supplement only those passages that had been modified, it would have been a fraction of its actual length, but he clearly wanted those reading the supplement to be able to appreciate the differences in context. Hence, rather than following the majority of editors by giving only the passages that are different in a series of variants, I have decided to give readers of the translation the possibility of a similar experience to the original readers, with the exception that they will be reading in the supplement not the original text, but the censored text. I have included a summary of which sections are involved and the changes made in an introduction to my new supplement in the appendix.

As far as the translation itself is concerned, I have not attempted to imitate eighteenth-century language, but have aimed for a contemporary style, making full use of contractions to aid fluency, but have nevertheless tried to avoid any obviously modern expressions.

As perhaps befits a translation that has preserved the French title of the play, I have adopted a foreignizing strategy in relation to the use of forms of address and other elements, such as Desparville *père*'s medal. These do not always have comfortable equivalents in the culture of the target language, but, even when they do, *Le Philosophe sans le savoir* is a play that is very much situated not only in a specific time, but also in a specific country, and the reader should be reminded of this.

Two other aspects of the play, both of which have a link to its status as a *drame*, are also potentially problematic for the translator, and so require some comment. First of all, the idea of family is very important in this genre, and this is reflected in the fact that, rather than using names, those characters who are related to each other make copious use of family relationships as forms of address. This is, of course, a common device in drama with large casts and complex plots to keep the audience informed about who is who, but that is clearly not Sedaine's intention here, for the cast is small enough and the plot simple enough for the audience to be able to follow easily. Rather he seems to be seeking to remind us of the importance of the bonds of family, something which even the comic Marquise recognizes, as she becomes besotted with her nephew and so forgets her initial desire for her relationship to her family to remain secret. This can sometimes feel unnatural in English, particularly as French always uses the possessive with the noun, as in 'mon père'; I have tried as far as possible to preserve this effect, but have often dropped the possessive, and have on one or two occasions preferred the bantering 'brother mine' to 'my brother'.

Secondly, Sedaine is an enthusiastic exponent of the exclamatory and fractured style advocated by Diderot to express emotion, so the text abounds in not only incomplete sentences, but also exclamatory words or syllables. The former is rarely a problem for the translator, but, in the case of the latter, a precise equivalent of the French original can often seem uncomfortable, so I have taken a very free approach to these, modifying them or omitting them as seemed sensible, and even, occasionally, adding them where the English text seemed to need something to underline the sense.

LE PHILOSOPHE
SANS LE SAVOIR,

COMEDY IN FIVE ACTS
IN PROSE,

Performed by the Comédiens Français ordinaires du Roi on 2 December 1765.

By M. SEDAINE.

SECOND EDITION.

DRAMATIS PERSONAE

CHARACTERS

M. VANDERK père,
M. VANDERK fils,
M. DESPARVILLE père, a former officer,
M. DESPARVILLE fils, a cavalry officer,
MME VANDERK,
A MARQUISE, the sister of M. Vanderk père,
ANTOINE, M. Vanderk's right-hand man,
VICTORINE, Antoine's daughter,
MLLE SOPHIE VANDERK, M. Vanderk's daughter,
A PRÉSIDENT, the fiancé of Mlle Vanderk,
A SERVANT of M. Desparville,
A SERVANT of M. Vanderk fils,
THE SERVANTS of the household,
THE SERVANT of the Marquise.

ACTORS

M. Brizard.[1]
M. Molé.[2]
M. Grandval.[3]
M. le Kain.[4]
Mlle Dumesnil.[5]
Mme Droüin.[6]
M. Préville.[7]
Mlle Doligny.[8]
Mlle Dépinai.[9]
M. Dauberval.[10]
M. Bouret.[11]
M. Auger.[12]
M. Feulie.[13]

---

[1] The stage name of Jean-Baptiste Britard (1721–1791). He was thought of mainly as a tragic actor; in non-tragic plays he tended to play the roles of fathers.
[2] François-René Molé (1734–1802) was a hugely popular actor, known particularly as an exponent of the emotional style of acting advocated by Diderot for the *drame*.
[3] Charles-François Racot de Grandval (1710–1784) was a playwright as well as an actor. He performed in tragedy and comedy.
[4] The stage name of Henri-Louis Caïn (1729–1778). One of the greatest tragic actors of his time, he campaigned along with Diderot to have spectators removed from the stage and for more natural styles of declamation and costumes.
[5] The stage name of Marie-Françoise Marchand (1713–1803). She specialized in roles of princesses and queens in tragedy.
[6] The stage name of Françoise-Marie-Jeanne-Elisabeth Gaultier (1720–1803). She was known for her versatility, but later in her career tended to specialize in character parts.
[7] The stage name of Pierre-Louis Dubus (1721–1799). He specialized in comic roles.
[8] The stage name of Louise-Adélaïde Berton-Maisonneuve (1746–1823). She specialized in comedy, but also took on the roles of young innocents in tragedy.
[9] The stage name of Pierrette Hélène Pinet (1740–1782), which she changed to Mademoiselle Molé when she married Molé in 1769. She generally played lovers in comedies and supporting roles in tragedies.
[10] The stage name of Étienne Dominique Bercher (1725–1800). He tended to take secondary roles.
[11] Antoine Claude Bouret (1732–1783) specialized in low comic roles.
[12] François Augé or Auger (1733–1783) specialized in the roles of valets in comedy.
[13] It is not clear why only a single actor is named to play multiple parts. Louis Henri Feulie (1736–1774) began his career specializing in playing valets.

The action takes place in a city in France.[14]

---

[14] In other words, not Paris. Sedaine would have had in mind one of the big commercial centres, and, given the importance of shipping for the merchant's trade, probably a major port. See on this matter H. T. Mason, who suggests Rouen as the most likely candidate ('*Le Philosophe sans le savoir*: An Aristocratic *Drame Bourgeois*', p. 406).

LE PHILOSOPHE SANS LE SAVOIR,
COMEDY.

ACT I.

A large study lit with candles and a desk covered in papers and boxes to one side.

SCENE I.

ANTOINE, VICTORINE.

ANTOINE.

What! I've found you with your handkerchief in your hand, looking embarrassed and drying your eyes, and you'll not tell me why you are crying?

VICTORINE.

Oh Father, young women sometimes cry to give themselves something to do.

ANTOINE.

I'll not be fobbed off with that explanation.

VICTORINE.

I was coming to ask you…

ANTOINE.

To ask me? And I'm asking you what reason you have to cry, and I'd like you to tell me.

VICTORINE.

You'll make fun of me.

ANTOINE.

There is certainly a risk of that.

VICTORINE.

But if what I have to tell you is true, you certainly wouldn't make fun.

ANTOINE.

Perhaps.

VICTORINE.

I went down to the cashier's office for Madame.

ANTOINE.

And?

VICTORINE.

There were a few gentlemen who were waiting their turn and who were talking to one another. One of them said: 'They drew their swords. We went out and separated them.'

ANTOINE.

Who?

VICTORINE.

That was what I asked. 'I don't know', one of them said to me, 'it was two young men, one a cavalry officer and the other in the navy'. 'Monsieur, did you see him?' 'Yes.' 'Did he have a blue jacket with red lapels and cuffs?' 'Yes.'[15] 'Was he young?' 'Yes, between twenty and twenty-two.' 'Handsome?' They smiled, I blushed, and I didn't dare carry on.

ANTOINE.

It's true that your questions were entirely appropriate for a modest young woman.

VICTORINE.

But if it were Monsieur's son?...

ANTOINE.

Is he the only person who's an officer?

VICTORINE.

That's what I thought.

ANTOINE.

Is he the only person in the navy?

---

[15] The omission of this 'Yes' in the second edition means that the rest of the dialogue becomes a little confused. I have corrected according to the first edition.

VICTORINE.

That's what I said to myself.

ANTOINE.

Is there no one but him who's young?

VICTORINE.

You're right.

ANTOINE.

You are very sensitive.

VICTORINE.

Another thing that makes me think it isn't him is that the man said that it was the navy officer who had started the argument.

ANTOINE.

But you were still crying.

VICTORINE.

Yes, I was crying.

ANTOINE.

You really have to like someone to become alarmed so easily.

VICTORINE.

But Father, after you, who do you think I should like more? After all, he's the son of the family; my poor mother was his wet nurse; we were brought up together;[16] he's the brother of my young mistress, and you are really fond of him.

ANTOINE.

I'm not saying you shouldn't like him, but be reasonable.

VICTORINE.

But it upset me.

---

[16] The original text says he is her 'frère de lait' ('milk brother'), a term that refers to the tradition that, despite the difference in social status, there is a particular bond between a child fed by a wet nurse and the wet nurse's own child.

ANTOINE.

Come on, you're being silly.

VICTORINE.

I hope so. But could you find out about it?

ANTOINE.

Where did they say the argument began?

VICTORINE.

In a café.

ANTOINE.

He never goes to them.

VICTORINE.

Perhaps he was there by chance. Oh, if I were a man, I'd go.

ANTOINE.

He'll be back any minute. And how could I find out in a big city…

SCENE II.

A SERVANT OF M. DESPARVILLE, ANTOINE, VICTORINE.

THE SERVANT.

Monsieur.

ANTOINE.

Can I help you?

THE SERVANT.

I have a letter to deliver to M. Vanderk.

ANTOINE.

You can leave it with me.

THE SERVANT.

I have to give it to him in person. My master gave me strict orders.

ANTOINE.

Monsieur isn't here, and, even if he were, you've chosen a bad time: it's late.

THE SERVANT.

It isn't nine yet.

ANTOINE.

Yes, but this evening they will be signing the marriage agreement of his daughter. If it's only a business letter, I'm his assistant, and I…

THE SERVANT.

I have to deliver it into his own hand.

ANTOINE.

In that case, go through into the shop and wait. I'll let you know when you can see him.

SCENE III.

ANTOINE, VICTORINE.

VICTORINE.

Monsieur isn't back?

ANTOINE.

No. He's gone back to the notary's.

VICTORINE.

Madame has sent me to ask you… Oh, I wish you could see Mademoiselle in her wedding outfit. She's just tried it on. The earrings, the necklace, a necklace all of diamonds. They're beautiful. There's one that's this big! And Mademoiselle: how lovely she is. Her fiancé is delighted. There he is, and he can't take his eyes off her. They've put some rouge on her, and a mouche here.[17] You wouldn't recognize her.

ANTOINE.

Well, not if she has a mouche!

---

[17] Mouches or patches were small fabric shapes that were stuck to the face to accentuate the whiteness of fashionably pale skin, or to cover blemishes caused by, for instance, smallpox or acne.

VICTORINE.

Madame said: 'Go and ask your father if Monsieur is back, if he's not busy with work, and if we can speak to him.' I'll tell you, but you mustn't say anything. Mademoiselle is going to have herself announced as an aristocratic lady under another name, and I'm sure that Monsieur will be taken in.

ANTOINE.

Oh, of course, a father won't recognize his own daughter.

VICTORINE.

No, he won't recognize her, I'm sure. When he arrives, let us know. It will be very funny… Still, it's not like him to be so late.

ANTOINE.

Who?

VICTORINE.

His son.

ANTOINE.

Are you still thinking about him?

VICTORINE.

I'm going. You'll let us know? Ah, here is Monsieur.

(*She leaves.*)

SCENE IV.

M. VANDERK *père*, TWO MEN *carrying baskets of money on their backs*, ANTOINE.

M. VANDERK père, turning, notices the porters and says to them:

Go to my cash office: down three steps, up five, and it's at the end of the corridor.

(*The porters leave.*)

ANTOINE.

I'll take them.

M. VANDERK *père*.

No, stay. The notaries are taking forever. (*He puts down his sword and his hat; he opens a desk.*) But after all, they're right. We think only of the present, and they think of the future. Is my son back?

ANTOINE.

No, Monsieur. Here are the rolls of twenty-five louis d'or that I got from the cash office.

M. VANDERK *père*.

Keep one. Oh, my poor Antoine, you're going to have a hard day tomorrow.

ANTOINE.

Make sure yours isn't harder than mine.

M. VANDERK *père*.

It will be hard enough.

ANTOINE.

Why? Leave everything to me.

M. VANDERK *père*.

You can't do everything.

ANTOINE.

I'll see to it all. Just think of yourself as someone who's been invited. You'll have quite enough to do in playing host to your guests.

M. VANDERK *père*.

You'll have a number of visiting servants, that's what worries me, particularly my sister's.

ANTOINE.

I know.

M. VANDERK *père*.

I don't want any bad behaviour.

ANTOINE.

There won't be any.

M. VANDERK *père*.

I want the clerks' table to be served just like mine.

ANTOINE.

Yes, Monsieur.

M. VANDERK *père*.

I'll go to see them.

ANTOINE.

I'll let them know.

M. VANDERK *père*.

I want to let them drink my health, and I'll drink to theirs.

ANTOINE.

They'll be honoured.

M. VANDERK *père*.

And not too much wine on the servants' table.

ANTOINE.

All right.

M. VANDERK *père*.

A half louis to each of them as a wedding gift. If you don't have enough, make it up yourself and I'll repay you.

ANTOINE.

All right.

M. VANDERK *père*.

I think that's everything… The shops should be closed: no one must go in after ten… Someone needs to stay in the offices and lock the door from the inside.

ANTOINE.

My daughter will stay.

M. VANDERK *père*.

No, your daughter must be with her friend. I've heard rumours of rockets and bangers. My son wants to get things going with a bang.

ANTOINE.

We can deal with that.

M. VANDERK *père*.

Still, make sure that the water tanks are full.

SCENE V.

VICTORINE, M. VANDERK *père*, ANTOINE.

(*Victorine comes in and whispers in her father's ear.*)

ANTOINE *to his daughter*.

Yes.

SCENE VI.

M. VANDERK *père*, ANTOINE.

ANTOINE.

Monsieur, do you think you are able to keep an important secret?

M. VANDERK *père*.

Are there more rockets? Some musicians?

ANTOINE.

No, something quite different. It's a young lady who has the greatest affection for you.

M. VANDERK *père*.

My daughter?

ANTOINE.

Exactly. She's asking to meet with you.

M. VANDERK *père*.

Do you know why?

ANTOINE.

She has been trying on her diamonds and her wedding dress, and they've put some rouge on her. She and Madame think that you won't recognize her. Here she is.

SCENE VII.

THE ACTORS FROM THE PREVIOUS SCENE, A SERVANT.

THE SERVANT.

Monsieur, Madame la Marquise de Vanderville.

M. VANDERK *père*.

Show her in.

(*The double doors are opened.*)

SCENE VIII.

M. VANDERK *père*, ANTOINE, Mlle SOPHIE VANDERK announced as Madame de Vanderville.

SOPHIE *curtseying low*.

Mon... Monsieur.

M. VANDERK *père*.

Madame. (*To the servant.*) Bring a chair. (*They sit.*) (*To Antoine.*) She's not bad. (*To Sophie.*) May I ask Madame why I have the honour of seeing her?

SOPHIE *trembling*.

It's because... Mon... Monsieur, I've... I've a document to give you.

M. VANDERK *père*.

I will be honoured if Madame wishes to entrust it to me.

(*While she is looking for it, he looks at Antoine.*)

ANTOINE.

Ah, Monsieur, how beautiful she is like that!

SOPHIE.

Here it is. (*The father gets up to take the document.*) Ah, Monsieur, don't trouble yourself. (*Aside.*) I can hardly speak.

M. VANDERK *père*.

That will be enough. It's thirty louis d'or. Perfect! (*While M. Vanderk is on his way to his desk, Sophie signals to Antoine not to say anything.*) This promissory note is excellent. It has come to you via Holland.

SOPHIE.

No… yes.

M. VANDERK *père*.

You are quite right, Madame… Here is the sum.

SOPHIE

Monsieur, I am your humble and obedient servant.

M. VANDERK *père*.

Madame isn't going to count it?

SOPHIE.

No. Ah! My dear Monsieur. You are such an honest man, that your reputation… you are so well known for…

SCENE IX.

THE ACTORS FROM THE PREVIOUS SCENE, MME VANDERK.

SOPHIE.

Ah, Mother, my dear father made fun of me.

M. VANDERK *père*.

What! You are my daughter?

SOPHIE.

Oh, you recognized me.

MME VANDERK *to her husband.*

What do you think of her?

M. VANDERK *père*.

She looks wonderful.

SOPHIE.

You didn't even look at me. I'm not deceitful. Here's your money that you give so trustingly to the first person that comes along.

M. VANDERK *père*.

Keep it. I don't want you ever to have to feel guilty of a falsehood even as a joke. I'm honouring your note. Keep the thirty louis d'or.

SOPHIE.

Dearest Father…

M. VANDERK *père*.

You'll have gifts to give tomorrow.

SCENE X.

THE ACTORS FROM THE PREVIOUS SCENE, THE FUTURE SON-IN-LAW.

M. VANDERK *père*.

Monsieur, you are about to marry quite a person. Having herself introduced under a false name, making use of a false signature to deceive her father: all that's just a joke to her.

THE SON-IN-LAW.

Ah, Monsieur, you have two guilty parties to punish. I'm her accomplice, and this is the hand that signed the note.

M. VANDERK *père taking the hands of his daughter and her fiancé.*

This is how I punish it.

THE SON-IN-LAW.

Then how would you reward it?

MME VANDERK.

(*Madame Vanderk signals to her daughter.*)

My daughter…

SOPHIE *to her fiancé.*

Monsieur, may I ask you...

THE SON-IN-LAW.

Whatever you say.

SOPHIE.

Guess what I want to say to you.

MME VANDERK *to her husband.*

Your daughter is feeling very awkward.

M. VANDERK *père.*

Why?

THE SON-IN-LAW *to Sophie.*

I wish I could guess what you want... Ah, it's to leave you alone?

SOPHIE.

Yes.

SCENE XI.

M. and MME VANDERK, SOPHIE.

MME VANDERK.

Your daughter is getting married tomorrow; she is leaving us. She wants to ask you...

M. VANDERK *père.*

Ah, Madame.

MME VANDERK *to her daughter.*

My daughter...

SOPHIE.

Mother!... Ah, dearest Father, I... (*She is about to fall to her knees; her father stops her.*)

M. VANDERK *père.*

My dear daughter, spare me and your mother the emotion of such a moment. All we have ever done has been intended simply to bring down on you and your brother all the blessings of Heaven. Never forget, dearest daughter, that the good conduct of parents is a blessing for their children.

SOPHIE.

I'll never forget it.

SCENE XII.

THE ACTORS FROM THE PREVIOUS SCENE, VICTORINE.

VICTORINE.

He's here, he's here.

MME VANDERK.

Who? Who then?

VICTORINE.

Monsieur your son.

MME VANDERK.

Victorine, I'm sure that the older you get, the odder you're getting.

VICTORINE.

Madame?

MME VANDERK.

First of all, in you come without being called.

VICTORINE.

But, Madame.

MME VANDERK.

Are we in the habit of announcing my son?

SOPHIE.

Really, my dear friend, you're quite mad.

VICTORINE.

But he's here.

SCENE XIII.

THE ACTORS FROM THE PREVIOUS SCENE, M. VANDERK *fils*.

SOPHIE.

Ah, now we'll see. (*M. Vanderk fils bows low to his sister, whom he does not recognize.*) Ah, my brother doesn't recognize me!

M. VANDERK *fils*.

Oh, it's my sister. She's beautiful!

MME VANDERK.

You find her pretty?

M. VANDERK *fils*.

Yes, Mother.

SCENE XIV.

THE ACTORS FROM THE PREVIOUS SCENE, THE SON-IN-LAW.

THE SON-IN-LAW *quietly to Sophie*.

Can I come in? The notaries… (*To the father.*) The notaries are here. (*He goes to give his arm to Sophie, who, smiling, points to her mother. He realizes his mistake.*) Ah!

SCENE XV.

M. VANDERK *fils*, SOPHIE, VICTORINE.

SOPHIE.

Do you think I look all right?

M. VANDERK *fils*.

Very much so.

SOPHIE.

And I think, brother mine, that it is very much not all right that on a day like today you've come home so late. Ask Victorine.

M. VANDERK *fils.*

What time is it, then?

SOPHIE *presenting him with a watch.*

Here. Look.

M. VANDERK *fils looking at the watch.*

It's true that it's a bit late; I think it's fast. It's nice. (*He tries to give it back to her.*)

SOPHIE.

No, I want you to keep it so that you'll feel eternally guilty that you kept us waiting.

M. VANDERK *fils.*

I accept it with all my heart. Every time I look at it, I'll feel better for knowing that you are happy.

SCENE XVI.

THE ACTORS FROM THE PREVIOUS SCENE, A SERVANT.

THE SERVANT *to Sophie.*

Mademoiselle, the company are expecting you.

SOPHIE.

Aren't you coming, my brother?

M. VANDERK *fils.*

Yes, I'll be there… soon. I'll follow you…

SCENE XVII.

M. VANDERK *fils*, VICTORINE.

VICTORINE.

I've been very worried about you. An argument in a café.

M. VANDERK *fils.*

Does my father know about it?

VICTORINE.

Is it true?

M. VANDERK *fils.*

No, no, Victorine.

(*He goes into the drawing room.*)

VICTORINE *leaving by another exit.*

Ah, I've been so worried.

End of Act I.

ACT II.

SCENE I.

ANTOINE, M. DESPARVILLE'S SERVANT.

ANTOINE.

Where on Earth were you?

THE SERVANT.

I was in the shop.

ANTOINE.

Who told you to go in there?

THE SERVANT.

You.

ANTOINE.

What? What were you doing there?

THE SERVANT.

Sleeping.

ANTOINE.

Sleeping! You must have been there more than three hours.

THE SERVANT.

I don't know about that. Anyway, is your master back?

ANTOINE.

Yes. They've even eaten.

THE SERVANT.

Well, can I give him my letter?

ANTOINE.

Wait.

SCENE II.

THE ACTORS FROM THE PREVIOUS SCENE, M. VANDERK *fils*.

THE SERVANT *seeing M. Vanderk fils come in.*

Isn't that him?

ANTOINE.

No, no, stay there. Goodness, you're a strange man to stay in that shop for three hours.

THE SERVANT.

To tell the truth, I would have been there all night, if I hadn't woken up hungry.

ANTOINE.

Come on, come on.

SCENE III.

M. VANDERK *fils alone*.

This is dreadful! I didn't want to go out. It was as if I had a premonition. A merchant... a merchant... It's my father's profession, after all, and I won't tolerate anyone insulting it. People may think I'm wrong, but... Oh, Father!... Father!... On a wedding day of all days! I can see all his worries, his pain, the despair of my mother, my sister, poor Victorine, and Antoine, the whole family. Lord, what wouldn't I do to go back a day, to go back... (*His father enters, and observes him.*) But no, I won't go back. Oh Lord!

(*He sees his father and assumes a cheerful manner.*)

SCENE IV.

M. VANDERK *père*, M. VANDERK *fils*.

M. VANDERK *père*.

Now Son, what can be the meaning of this agitation and bad temper?

M. VANDERK *fils*.

I was making a speech; I was being heroic.

M. VANDERK *père*.

You wouldn't be putting on some play tomorrow, a tragedy perhaps, would you?

M. VANDERK *fils*.

No, no, Father.

M. VANDERK *père*.

Go ahead, if it amuses you, but some precautions will be needed. Tell me, and if it's important that I don't know, I won't know.

M. VANDERK *fils*.

I'm very grateful, Father. I'll tell you.

M. VANDERK *père*.

Take care. If you don't tell me the truth, I'll come and heckle.

M. VANDERK *fils*.

I'm not worried about that. But, Father, the marriage contract of my sister has just been read; we've all signed it. What name did you use? And what name did you make me use?

M. VANDERK *père*.

Yours.

M. VANDERK *fils*.

Mine! Is the name I use?...

M. VANDERK *père*.

It's only an assumed name.

M. VANDERK *fils*.

You called yourself Chevalier, erstwhile Baron of Savières, of Clavières, of…

M. VANDERK *père*.

And I am.

M. VANDERK *fils*.

So you're a nobleman?

M. VANDERK *père*.

Yes.

M. VANDERK *fils*.

Yes!

M. VANDERK *père*.

Don't you believe me?

M. VANDERK *fils*.

Yes, Father. But is it possible?...

M. VANDERK *père*.

You don't think it's possible that I might be a nobleman?

M. VANDERK *fils*.

I'm not saying that. But is it possible that, even if you were the poorest of nobles, you would have taken a trade?...

M. VANDERK *père*.

Son, when a man enters the world, he is the plaything of circumstances.

M. VANDERK *fils*.

Are there any circumstances serious enough to make us abandon the highest of ranks for the?...

M. VANDERK *père*.

Go on: for the lowest.

M. VANDERK *fils*.

That's not what I meant.

M. VANDERK *père*.

Listen: the most important thing a father can pass on to his son is the honour that he has inherited from his ancestors. Sit down. (*He sits; the son takes a chair, but does not sit down.*) I was brought up by your grandfather; my father was very young when he was killed leading his regiment. If you were less sensible, I wouldn't tell you the story of my youth. This is it. Your mother, the daughter of a nobleman who was our neighbour, was the only woman I ever loved. At an age when you don't really choose who you fall in love with, I was fortunate enough to choose well. A young officer who was quartered for the winter in the area disapproved of the fact that a child of sixteen like me was attracting the attention of another child, your mother was only twelve, and he treated me with an arrogance that I couldn't tolerate. We fought.

M. VANDERK *fils*.

You fought?

M. VANDERK *père*.

Yes, Son.

M. VANDERK *fils*.

With pistols?

M. VANDERK *père*.

No, with swords. I was forced to leave the region. Your mother swore to be faithful to me, and she has been for her whole life. I took ship. A worthy Dutchman, the owner of the vessel I was on, took a shine to me. We were attacked, and I was of use to him. (It was there that I got to know Antoine.) The kind Dutchman took me into his business; he offered me his niece and his fortune. I told him of my attachment; he approved. Off he went; he obtained the consent of your mother's parents, and he brought her back to me with her nursemaid. (She is the good old woman who is here with us.) We were married. The good Dutchman died in my arms, and at his request I took his name and his business. Fate has been good to me, and I can't be happier. I am respected. Here is your sister well established: your brother-in-law is the honourable holder of one of the most important posts in the law. And you, my son, will be a worthy successor to me and to your ancestors. I have already restored to our family all the assets that the necessity of serving the prince had caused our forebears to lose. Those assets will be yours. And if you think that by becoming a businessman I have caused a stain on their name, it is up to you to remove it. But in a century as enlightened as this one, what can bestow nobility is not capable of removing it.[18]

M. VANDERK *fils*.

Ah, Father, I don't think that, but unfortunately the prejudice is so strong…

M. VANDERK *père*.

Prejudice? Such a prejudice is nothing in the eyes of reason.

---

[18] In order to encourage trade, it had long been possible for members of the noblity to operate as merchants without losing their noble status, but entrenched attitudes meant that this was of limited success, so the next move was to allow successful merchants to become ennobled. For further information on this, see Mason, '*Le Philosophe sans le savoir*: An Aristocratic *Drame Bourgeois?*', pp. 407–08.

M. VANDERK *fils*.

That doesn't change the fact that the status of a businessman is seen as…

M. VANDERK *père*.

What is the status, Son, of a man who, with a stroke of his pen, can ensure that he is obeyed from one end of the universe to the other? Monarchs need the value of metal to serve as security for their currency, but his name, his signature have no need of that; he himself is sufficient. He has signed, and that is enough.

M. VANDERK *fils*.

I agree, but…

M. VANDERK *père*.

It is not one race, it is not a single nation that he serves, he serves them all, and he is served by them. He is a man of the universe.

M. VANDERK *fils*.

That may be true, but in himself, what is respectable about him?

M. VANDERK *père*.

Respectable! The same that legitimizes in a nobleman the rights of his birth, and forms the basis of his titles: honesty, honour, and integrity.

M. VANDERK *fils*.

Your conduct alone, Father…

M. VANDERK *père*.

A few bold individuals cause kings to arm themselves, war breaks out, violence erupts, Europe is divided, but the English, Dutch, Russian, or Chinese merchant is no less my soulmate. We are so many silken threads across the surface of the Earth who link the nations together and restore them to peace through the need for commerce. That, my son, is what an honest merchant is.

M. VANDERK *fils*.

And the nobleman, then, and the soldier?

M. VANDERK *père*.

I know of only two professions above the merchant (always supposing that there is any difference between those who do the best they can in the role fate has placed them in), two professions, the magistrate, who is the voice of the law, and the soldier, who defends his homeland.

M. VANDERK *fils*.

So I'm a nobleman?

M. VANDERK *père*.

Yes, my son. There are few good families to whom you are not connected and who are not connected to you.

M. VANDERK *fils*.

So why have you kept it from me?

M. VANDERK *père*.

It was perhaps a needless precaution; I was afraid that pride in a great name would become the source of your qualities, and I wanted them to come from you yourself. Until now I have spared you the remarks you've just made, remarks that at a younger age would have been expressed with more bitterness.

M. VANDERK *fils*.

I don't think that I ever…

SCENE V.

THE ACTORS FROM THE PREVIOUS SCENE, ANTOINE, M. DESPARVILLE'S SERVANT.

M. VANDERK *père*.

What is it?

ANTOINE.

He's been here for more than three hours, Monsieur. He's a servant.

M. VANDERK *père*.

Why have you made him wait? Why didn't you let him deliver his message? His time might be precious; his master may need him.

ANTOINE.

I forgot about him; we ate, and he fell asleep.

THE SERVANT.

I fell asleep. Heavens, I'm tired, tired…. Where on Earth is it now? That damned letter will be the death of me today.

M. VANDERK père.

Take your time.

THE SERVANT.

Ah, here it is!

(*While the father reads, the servant yawns, and the son is lost in thought.*)

M. VANDERK père.

Say to your master... Who is your master?

THE SERVANT.

Monsieur Desparville.

M. VANDERK père.

I understand. But what does he do?

THE SERVANT.

I haven't been with him long, but he served.

M. VANDERK père.

Served?

THE SERVANT.

Yes, he has the cross. It's blue, it has a blue ribbon.[19] It's not like the others, but it's the same thing.

M. VANDERK père.

Tell your master, tell M. Desparville, that I'll be here at his service tomorrow between three and four in the afternoon.

THE SERVANT.

I will.

M. VANDERK père.

And please tell him that I am very sorry not to be able to give him an earlier appointment; I am very tied up.

---

[19] This is an indication that the character is a Protestant. Protestants were not allowed to receive the cross of Saint Louis, with its red ribbon, but were instead awarded the Ordre du Mérite Militaire (the Order of Military Merit), which had a blue ribbon.

THE SERVANT.

I know, I know.

(*As the servant turns towards the shop, Antoine says:*)

Hey, where are you going? To go back to sleep!

SCENE VI.

M. VANDERK *père*, M. VANDERK *fils*.

M. VANDERK *fils*.

Father, please forgive me for what I said.

M. VANDERK *père*.

It's better to speak out than to keep it to yourself.

M. VANDERK *fils*.

But perhaps I was too forthright.

M. VANDERK *père*.

That's typical at your age. You are going to meet a woman who is much more forthright than you on that front. Unless you're a soldier, you're nothing.

M. VANDERK *fils*.

Who is that?

M. VANDERK *père*.

Your aunt, my own sister. She should have arrived. I achieved nothing by setting her up honourably. She is now a widow without children. She benefits from all the revenue from the assets I bought for you; I've lavished on her everything that I thought would satisfy her whims; nevertheless, she will never forgive me for the profession I've adopted, and whilst my gifts don't soil her hands, the name of Brother would soil her lips. Still, she is the best of women, but this is how giving in to prejudice stifles natural affection and gratitude.

M. VANDERK *fils*.

If I were in your position, Father, I would never forgive her.

M. VANDERK *père*.

Why not? That's how she is, Son. It's a weakness she has. It may be a misplaced sense of honour, but it's a sense of honour nonetheless.

M. VANDERK *fils.*

You've never mentioned this aunt to me before.

M. VANDERK *père.*

That silence was part of the way I decided to bring you up. She lives in deepest darkest Berry, where she upholds rather too imperiously the name of our ancestors, and her idea of nobility is so strong that I wouldn't have been able to persuade her to come to your sister's wedding if I hadn't written that she is marrying a gentleman. Even then, she has imposed some strange conditions.

M. VANDERK *fils.*

Conditions!

M. VANDERK *père.*

'My dear brother', she writes, 'I will attend, but would it not be better if I passed as only a distant relative of your wife, as a benefactress of the family?' She backs that up with all the flawed reasoning that… I can hear a carriage.

M. VANDERK *fils.*

I'll go and see.

SCENE VII.

THE ACTORS FROM THE PREVIOUS SCENE, MME VANDERK, SOPHIE, THE SON-IN-LAW, VICTORINE.

MME VANDERK.

I think this is my sister-in-law.

M. VANDERK *père.*

We'll see.

SOPHIE.

Here's my aunt.

M. VANDERK *père.*

Stay here. I'll go and meet her.

THE SON-IN-LAW.

Should I come with you?

M. VANDERK *père*.

No, stay. Victorine, light my way.

(*Victorine takes a candle and goes ahead.*)

SCENE VIII.

MME VANDERK, M. VANDERK *fils*, SOPHIE, THE SON-IN-LAW.

THE SON-IN-LAW.

So, my dear brother, you're looking a little serious today.

M. VANDERK *fils*.

No, not at all.

THE SON-IN-LAW.

Are you afraid that your dear sister won't be happy with me?

M. VANDERK *fils*.

I'm sure she will be.

SOPHIE *to her mother*.

Should I call her Aunt?

MME VANDERK.

Be very careful not to. Leave it to me to speak.

SCENE IX.

THE ACTORS FROM THE PREVIOUS SCENE, M. VANDERK *père*, VICTORINE, THE AUNT, A LACKEY OF THE AUNT *in a waistcoat, with a silk belt, boots, and with a whip over his shoulder, carrying the train of his mistress's dress.*

THE AUNT.

Ah, I'm dazzled. Take away those candles. There is no order on the roads; I should have been here two hours ago. Whether you are of the nobility or not, a duchess or the wife of a financier, it's all the same. Terrible horses; my women have had such frights. (*To her lackey.*) You, let go of my dress. Ah, it's Madame Vanderk!

MME VANDERK *comes forward, greets her, and puts on a dignified air.*

Madame, I have the honour of introducing my daughter to you.

THE AUNT *keeps her distance by curtseying rather than embracing Sophie.*

Who is this gentleman in black, and this young man?

M. VANDERK *père.*

It's my future son-in-law.

THE AUNT *looking at the son.*

You only have to look at him to see that he is of noble blood.

M. VANDERK *père.*

Don't you think that he has a ressemblance to Grandfather?

THE AUNT.

Well... Yes... the forehead. No doubt he is well on in his military career?

M. VANDERK *père.*

No, he is too young.

THE AUNT.

But, of course, he is attached to a regiment.

M. VANDERK *père.*

No.

THE AUNT.

Why not?

M. VANDERK *père.*

When by his services he has earned the favour of court, I will be ready.

THE AUNT.

You have your reasons. He is very fine... No doubt your daughter loves him?

M. VANDERK *père.*

Yes, they are very fond of each other.

THE AUNT.

But I would not be particularly concerned by that love, and I would have wanted my son-in-law to have a rank before giving him my daughter.

M. VANDERK *père*.

He is a président.

THE AUNT.

A président! Why is he carrying a sword?

M. VANDERK *père*.

Who? This is my future son-in-law.

THE AUNT.

Him? So Monsieur is in the law?

THE SON-IN-LAW.

Yes, Madame, and very proud to be.

THE AUNT.

Monsieur, in the law there are people who are connected to the best.

THE SON-IN-LAW.

And who are the best, Madame.

THE AUNT.

(*To her brother.*) You didn't say in your letter that he was in the law. (*To the son-in-law.*) My compliments to you, Monsieur, I am charmed to see you become part of a family…

THE SON-IN-LAW.

Madame.

THE AUNT.

Of a family in which I take the keenest interest.

THE SON-IN-LAW.

Madame.

THE AUNT.

Mademoiselle's whole being has an aura, a grace, a modesty, a seriousness. She will be a worthy wife to Monsieur le Président. (*Looking at the son.*) And this young man?

M. VANDERK *père*.

This is my son.

THE AUNT.

Your son! Your son! You aren't telling me... You aren't telling me this is my nephew. Ah, he's charming, he's charming. Embrace me, my dear child. Oh, you are right, he's the very image of Grandfather. He's struck me, his eyes, his forehead, his noble mien. Ah, my brother, ah, Monsieur, I want to take him with me, I want to show him off at home; I'll present him. Ah, he's charming.

MME VANDERK.

Madame, would you like to go to your rooms?

M. VANDERK *père*.

We'll have something brought for you to eat.

THE AUNT.

Oh, I want my bed. My bed and some clear soup. Ah, he's charming. I'm reserving him to take my arm tomorrow. Goodnight, my dear nephew, goodnight.

M. VANDERK *fils*.

My dear aunt, I wish you a...

SCENE X.

M. VANDERK *fils*, VICTORINE.

M. VANDERK *fils*.

My dear aunt is quite mad.

VICTORINE.

Madame is your aunt?

M. VANDERK *fils*.

Yes, my father's sister.

VICTORINE.

Her servants make quite an entourage. She has four or five, not counting the women. And they are so arrogant. Madame la Marquise here, Madame la Marquise there; she wants this, she intends that. It's as if everything belongs to them.

M. VANDERK *fils*.

That doesn't surprise me.

VICTORINE.

You aren't going with her, your dear aunt?

M. VANDERK *fils*.

I'm going. Goodnight, Victorine.

VICTORINE.

No, wait.

M. VANDERK *fils*.

What do you want?

VICTORINE.

Let me see your new watch.

M. VANDERK *fils*.

You haven't seen it?

VICTORINE.

Let me see it again!... Oh, it's beautiful... diamonds... a repeater.... It's eleven o'clock, seven, eight, nine, ten minutes, ten past eleven. At this time tomorrow… Do you want me to tell you all that you're going to be doing tomorrow?

M. VANDERK *fils*.

What I'm going to be doing?

VICTORINE.

Yes... You'll get up at seven, or say eight o'clock; you'll come down at ten; you'll give your arm to the bride; we'll get back at two o'clock; we'll dine and play cards; then we'll have your firework display, providing that you aren't hurt.

M. VANDERK *fils*.

Hurt? What does that matter?

VICTORINE.

You mustn't be.

M. VANDERK *fils*.

All right!

VICTORINE.

I'll wager that's everything you'll do tomorrow.

M. VANDERK *fils*.

You'd be very surprised if I didn't do any of that.

VICTORINE.

So, what would you do?

M. VANDERK *fils*.

Anyway, you may well be right.

VICTORINE.

It's a clever thing, a repeater watch. When you wake up, you can make it chime the hour. I think I'd wake up specially.

M. VANDERK *fils*.

All right, I want it to spend the night in your room, to find out if you wake yourself up.

VICTORINE.

Oh no!

M. VANDERK *fils*.

Please.

VICTORINE.

If anyone knew, they'd make fun of me.

M. VANDERK *fils*.

Who will tell them? You can give it back to me tomorrow morning.

VICTORINE.

You can be sure of it. But... what about you?

M. VANDERK *fils*.

I have my clock, haven't I? And you'll give it back.

VICTORINE.

Of course.

M. VANDERK *fils*.

Only to me.

VICTORINE.

Who else would I give it to?

M. VANDERK *fils*.

Only to me.

VICTORINE.

Yes, of course.

M. VANDERK *fils*.

Goodnight, Victorine... Goodbye... Goodnight. Only to me, only to me.

SCENE XI.

VICTORINE *alone*.

Only to me, only to me, what does he mean? There is something strange about him today. He doesn't have his usual cheerfulness, his open manner. He was lost in his thoughts. If it was... No.

SCENE XII.

ANTOINE, VICTORINE.

ANTOINE *to his daughter*.

They are calling for you. They've been ringing for an hour.

(*Victorine leaves.*)

SCENE XIII.

ANTOINE *alone.*

Four or five wretched lackeys from a noble residence are more trouble than a household of forty people. We'll see tomorrow… There will be quite an uproar… I haven't forgotten anything? No. (*He blows the candles out and closes the shutters.*) I'm off to bed.

SCENE XIV.

ONE OF M. VANDERK'S SERVANTS, ANTOINE.

ANTOINE.

What is it?

THE SERVANT.

Monsieur Antoine, Monsieur says that before you go to bed you should go up to see him by the small staircase.

ANTOINE.

All right. I'm on my way.

THE SERVANT.

Goodnight, Monsieur Antoine.

ANTOINE.

Goodnight, goodnight.

End of Act II.

ACT III.

SCENE I.

M. VANDERK fils and HIS SERVANT enter feeling their way carefully; he has the shutter that was closed by Antoine the previous evening opened to find out if it has begun to get light. He looks all around.[20]

(He should be in a riding coat and boots.)

SCENE II.

M. VANDERK fils, HIS SERVANT, he is wearing boots like his master.

M. VANDERK *fils.*

Champagne,[21] open the shutter... So, the keys?

THE SERVANT.

I looked everywhere, on the window sill, behind the door; I felt right along the iron bar that secures the door; I've not found anything. Eventually I woke up the porter.

---

[20] This opening stage direction is somewhat confusing, as, in order to explain what is going on, it apparently anticipates what is going to happen at the beginning of the next scene. The most likely intention is that Vanderk *fils* enters alone and looks around him, then the change of scene signals the subsequent entry of the servant. The action is perhaps clearer in the first edition, which has no change of scene, although here both characters enter together:

SCENE I.

M. VANDERK *fils*, HIS SERVANT.

M. Vanderk fils enters feeling his way carefully; the servant opens the shutter closed by Antoine the previous evening. M. Vanderk fils looks all around. The servant is wearing boots, as is his master, who is carrying a pair of pistols.

M. VANDERK *fils.*

So, the keys?

[21] This is, of course, the name of the servant, not a reference to the sparkling wine. Such regional names were frequently given to servants by their masters, sometimes, but not always, deriving from the servant's region of origin.

M. VANDERK *fils*.

And?

THE SERVANT.

He says that Monsieur Antoine has them.

M. VANDERK *fils*.

And why has Antoine taken the keys?

THE SERVANT.

I've no idea.

M. VANDERK *fils*.

Does he usually take them?

THE SERVANT.

I didn't ask. Do you want me to go and find out?

M. VANDERK *fils*.

No. And our horses?

THE SERVANT.

They are in the courtyard.

M. VANDERK *fils*.

Here, attach these pistols to the saddle, and don't fiddle with them. Have you heard any noise in the house?

THE SERVANT.

No. Everyone's asleep. But I did see some light.

M. VANDERK *fils*.

Where?

THE SERVANT.

On the third floor.

M. VANDERK *fils*.

The third floor?

THE SERVANT.

Ah! It's in Mademoiselle Victorine's room. It's her lamp.

M. VANDERK *fils*.

Victorine… Off you go.

THE SERVANT.

Where am I going?

M. VANDERK *fils*.

Down into the courtyard. Listen, hide the horses under the left-hand shelter next to my mother's carriage. Above all, be quiet; we mustn't wake anyone.

SCENE III.

M. VANDERK *fils alone*.

Why has Antoine taken those keys? What am I going to do? I'll have to wake him up. I'll say to him… I want to go out… There are things I need to buy, things I need to sort out… Let's knock. Antoine… I can't hear anything… Antoine… (*On the point of knocking, he stops himself.*) He's going to ask me a hundred questions. You're very early going out. What is it you need to sort out, then? You're going on horseback; wait till it's light. I don't want to wait… Give me the keys. (*He knocks.*) Antoine.

SCENE IV.

M. VANDERK *fils*, ANTOINE *in his room*.

ANTOINE.

Who's there?

M. VANDERK *fils*.

He's answered. Antoine.

ANTOINE.

Who can be knocking so early?

M. VANDERK *fils*.

Me.

ANTOINE.

Ah, Monsieur! I'm coming.

SCENE V.

M. VANDERK *fils* alone.

He's getting up… It's the most natural thing in the world: I've got things to do, I'm going out. I'm just going round the corner; why would I be going any further? But you're wearing boots. What about that horse, this servant? Well, I'm going two leagues away. My father asked me to run an errand for him. How hard the mind has to search for the simplest of reasons. Ah, I don't know how to lie.

SCENE VI.

M. VANDERK *fils*, ANTOINE, *his collar in his hand.*

ANTOINE.

What, Monsieur, it's you?

M. VANDERK *fils*.

Yes. Quickly, give me the keys to the porte cochère.

ANTOINE.

The keys?

M. VANDERK *fils*.

Yes.

ANTOINE.

The keys? But the porter should have them.

M. VANDERK *fils*.

He says you have them.

ANTOINE.

Oh, he's right. Yesterday evening, I'd forgotten. But in fact, Monsieur your father has them.

M. VANDERK *fils*.

My father. And why does he have them?

ANTOINE.

Ask him. I have no idea.

M. VANDERK *fils*.

He doesn't usually have them.

ANTOINE.

But you're going out very early.

M. VANDERK *fils*.

He must have had some reason for taking those keys.

ANTOINE.

Some servant, perhaps. This wedding... He's been dreading problems, revelry, aubades... He wants to be up first. I really don't know.

M. VANDERK *fils*.

All right, dearest Antoine, do me a huge... do me a small favour. Go into my father's apartment very quietly, please. He'll have put the keys on some table or chair. Bring them to me. Make sure you don't wake him. I'd be very upset to be the reason for his sleep being disturbed.

ANTOINE.

Why don't you go?

M. VANDERK *fils*.

If he hears you, you'll think of an excuse better than me.

ANTOINE.

I'll go. Stay here, stay here.

SCENE VII.

M. VANDERK *fils alone*.

Where do you think I might go?... I thought he might have asked me more questions. Antoine is a good man... He'll be thinking... Ah, Father, Father!... He's asleep... He doesn't know... This office... this house, everything I can see means more to me; to leave it for ever, or for a long time, causes me pain that... Here he comes... Heavens, it's my father!

SCENE VIII.

M. VANDERK *père in his dressing gown,* M. VANDERK *fils.*

M. VANDERK *fils.*

Father, I'm really annoyed. It's Antoine's fault. I told him, but he must have made a noise and woken you.

M. VANDERK *père.*

No, I was already awake.

M. VANDERK *fils.*

You were? And presumably…

M. VANDERK *père.*

Aren't you going to say good morning to me?

M. VANDERK *fils.*

Sorry, Father. I wish you a good morning. How did you sleep? How are you?

M. VANDERK *père.*

You're going out early.

M. VANDERK *fils.*

Yes, I wanted to…

M. VANDERK *père.*

There are horses in the courtyard.

M. VANDERK *fils.*

They're for me. They're mine and my servant's.

M. VANDERK *père.*

And where are you going so early?

M. VANDERK *fils.*

A sudden desire for some exercise. I wanted to go round the ramparts. An idea… a whim that I felt all of a sudden this morning.

M. VANDERK *père*.

You had already given orders to have your horses ready yesterday evening. Victorine heard it from someone, one of the stable hands, and you were intending to go out.

M. VANDERK *fils*.

It wasn't definite.

M. VANDERK *père*.

No, Son, you have some plan.

M. VANDERK *fils*.

What plan do you think I might have?

M. VANDERK *père*.

I'm asking you.

M. VANDERK *fils*.

Believe me, Father…

M. VANDERK *père*.

My son, until this moment, I've never known you to be evasive or to lie. If what you are telling me is true, say it to me again, and I'll believe you… If it's a matter of the sort of reasons, those follies that are the result of your age, the silliness that a father might suspect, but should never know about, whatever pain that might cause me, I'm not insisting that you confide something that would make us both blush. Here are the keys. Go… (*The son holds out his hand and takes them.*) But, Son, if it is something that will go on to cause problems for you, and for me and your mother…

M. VANDERK *fils*.

Oh, Father!

M. VANDERK *père*.

It isn't possible that there might be anything dishonourable in what you are going to do?

M. VANDERK *fils*.

Oh, rather…

M. VANDERK *père.*

Carry on.

M. VANDERK *fils.*

You don't know what you're asking! Oh, Father, you told me yesterday how you had been insulted; you were young, you fought; you would do it again... I'm so miserable! I have the feeling that I'm going to cause the greatest misfortune of your life. No... Never... What a lesson!... You can believe me... If fate...

M. VANDERK *père.*

Insulted... Fought... The greatest misfortune of my life. Son, let's talk, and look on me as just a friend.

M. VANDERK *fils.*

If it were possible that I might insist on one thing from you... Promise me that, whatever I have to tell you, your kindness won't stop me doing what I must do.

M. VANDERK *père.*

If it's just.

M. VANDERK *fils.*

Just or not.

M. VANDERK *père.*

Or not?

M. VANDERK *fils.*

Don't be alarmed. Yesterday evening I had an argument, a dispute with a cavalry officer. We went outside. We were separated... We have given our word to meet today.

M. VANDERK *père, supporting himself on the back of a chair.*

Oh, my son!

M. VANDERK *fils.*

Father, this is what I was afraid of.

M. VANDERK *père with strength.*

I am far from trying to stop you doing what you must, (*painfully*) you are an officer, and when you have made a commitment in public, you must honour it, however it may go against common sense or even nature.

M. VANDERK *fils*.

I don't need to be reminded.

M. VANDERK *père*.

I believe you. And will you tell me about your quarrel in more detail and what caused it; in fact, everything that happened?

M. VANDERK *fils*.

Ah, I've done everything I could to avoid seeing you.

M. VANDERK *père*.

Does it upset you?

M. VANDERK *fils*.

Never, never have I needed a friend so much, you in particular.

M. VANDERK *père*.

So, you had an argument.

M. VANDERK *fils*.

It's not a long story. The rain we had yesterday forced me to go into a café. I was playing a game of chess. I heard someone quite close to me talking heatedly. He was telling some story or other about his father, about a merchant, and fees charged on promissory notes. But I'm certain that I heard quite distinctly: 'Yes, all these merchants, all these businessmen are rogues and scoundrels.' I turned round and looked at him. Without any attention or regard for who might hear him, he repeated what he'd just said. I got up; I said in his ear that only a dishonest man could make such comments. We went outside. We were separated.

M. VANDERK *père*.

Will you allow me to say…

M. VANDERK *fils*.

Oh, Father, I know all the objections you can make. The officer might have been having a moment of bad temper; what he was saying might have had nothing to do with me; when you say everybody, you don't mean anybody; it's even possible he was only repeating what someone else had said to him. And this is why I'm tormented with grief. I've been tortured by my soul-searching. I must try to kill someone who may not be in the wrong. Still, I believe he said it, because I was there.

M. VANDERK *père*.

That's what you want to believe. Does he know you?

M. VANDERK *fils*.

I don't know him.

M. VANDERK *père*.

And you have sought a quarrel? There is nothing I can advise you.

M. VANDERK *fils*.

Father, be calm.

M. VANDERK *père*.

Oh, Son, why did you not think that you had a father? I so often think that I have a son.

M. VANDERK *fils*.

It's because I thought that.

M. VANDERK *père, after giving a deep sigh.*

What sword do you have with you?

M. VANDERK *fils*.

I have my pistols.

M. VANDERK *père*.

Your pistols? The weapon of a gentleman is his sword.

M. VANDERK *fils*.

He chose.

M. VANDERK *père*.

And into what uncertainty, what pain were you throwing me and your mother today!

M. VANDERK *fils*.

I'd seen to that.

M. VANDERK *père*.

How?

M. VANDERK *fils*.

I'd left on my table a letter addressed to you. Victorine would have given it to you.

M. VANDERK *père*.

Did you confide in Victorine?

M. VANDERK *fils*.

No, but she had to put something back on my table, and she would have seen it.

M. VANDERK *père*.

And what precautions have you taken against the legitimate force of the law?

M. VANDERK *fils*.

To go on the run.

M. VANDERK *père*.

Go back up to your apartment and bring me that letter; I'm going to write to assure your safety. May Heaven preserve you. Can one ask such a thing for a murder, for two perhaps?

M. VANDERK *fils*.

How miserable I am!

M. VANDERK *père*.

Go by your mother's apartment. Tell her... No, it's better if she doesn't see you for another twelve hours. Oh God!

SCENE IX.

M. VANDERK *père*.

What a misfortune! How fragile our present happiness is. I went to bed the most peaceful and happiest of fathers, and look at me now! (*He sits at his desk and writes.*) Antoine. I can't be too confident. (*Antoine enters.*) Ah, as long as I see him again. (*He writes.*) If he were to shed his blood for his king and country, but...

SCENE X.

M. VANDERK *père*, ANTOINE.

ANTOINE.

What is it you want?

M. VANDERK *père*.

What I want? That he lives.

ANTOINE.

Monsieur?

M. VANDERK *père*.

I didn't hear you come in.

ANTOINE.

You called me.

M. VANDERK *père*.

Antoine, I know your discretion, your friendship for me and for my son. He is going out to fight.

ANTOINE.

Who with? I'm going.

M. VANDERK *père*.

There's no point.

ANTOINE.

Everyone in the area will defend him. I'll go and wake them up.

M. VANDERK *père*.

No, that's not what…

ANTOINE.

You'll have to kill me rather than…

M. VANDERK *père*.

Quiet, he's still here. He's coming; leave us.

SCENE XI.

M. VANDERK *père*, M. VANDERK *fils*.

M. VANDERK *fils*.

I'll read it to you.

M. VANDERK *père*.

No, give it to me. And what are your plans? The place, the time?

M. VANDERK *fils*.

I only wanted to go out so early so that I didn't break my word: I was afraid of the fuss of today, and of finding myself tied up so that I couldn't escape. How I wish it could have been a day later.

M. VANDERK *père*.

Well?

M. VANDERK *fils*.

Three in the afternoon. We're meeting behind the low ramparts.

M. VANDERK *père*.

And couldn't you have stayed here from now to three o'clock?

M. VANDERK *fils*.

Father! Just think.

M. VANDERK *père*.

You are right, I wasn't thinking. Here, these are letters for Calais and for England. You'll have replacement horses. I just hope you'll need them!

M. VANDERK *fils*.

Father.

M. VANDERK *père*.

Oh, my son! People are starting to move around in the house. Goodbye.

M. VANDERK *fils*.

Goodbye, Father. Embrace for me…

(*His father pushes him away lovingly, and does not embrace him. The son takes a few steps to leave, then turns and holds his arms out to his father, who indicates he should go.*)

SCENE XII.

M. VANDERK *père*.

Oh, my son! To trample on reason, nature, and the law. What a fatal prejudice! This cruel abuse of the point of honour could only have been born in the most barbaric era. It could survive only in the midst of a nation that is vain and full of itself, amidst a people in which each individual thinks he is everything, and his country and family nothing. And you, wise yet inadequate laws, you wanted to put a curb on honour; you have ennobled the scaffold; your severity has meant that the heart of a decent man is torn between disgrace and execution. Oh, my son!

SCENE XIII.

M. VANDERK *père*, ANTOINE.

ANTOINE.

You've let him go.

M. VANDERK *père*.

No one here must find out about this.

ANTOINE.

It is already light in Madame's apartment, and if he went to see her…

M. VANDERK *père*.

He's gone. Ah, Heavens! Come with me, I'm going to get dressed.

End of Act III.

ACT IV.

SCENE I.

VICTORINE *alone.*

I'm searching all over for him. What's happened to him? I don't understand. He'll never be ready on time. He isn't dressed. Oh, I'm really annoyed that I can't give back his watch. All night I saw him saying 'Only to me, only to me, only to me'. He went out very early, and on horseback. What if it was that argument, and if it was true that he'd gone to… Oh, I have a premonition. But what would I risk by mentioning it? I'm going to tell Monsieur about it. I'd wager it was that servant who fell asleep here yesterday evening. I didn't like the look of his face. He must have arranged a meeting. Ah!

SCENE II.

M. VANDERK *père*, VICTORINE.

VICTORINE.

Monsieur, we are very worried. Madame la Marquise is saying, 'Is my nephew dressed? Go and warn him. Is he ready? Why haven't I seen him? Why isn't he here?'

M. VANDERK *père*.

You mean my son?

VICTORINE.

Yes. I've enquired about him, I've sent people to look for him; I don't know if he's gone out or if he hasn't gone out, but I haven't found him.

M. VANDERK *père*.

He's gone out.

VICTORINE.

So you know, Monsieur, that he's out?

M. VANDERK *père*.

Yes, I know. Go and see if everyone is ready. I am. Where is your father?

Le Philosophe sans le savoir

VICTORINE *takes a step, and comes back.*

Yesterday, Monsieur, did you see a servant who wanted to speak to you or to Monsieur your son?

M. VANDERK *père.*

A servant? It was for me. I've arranged a meeting with his master today. You've done well to remind me of it.

VICTORINE *aside.*

Thank goodness it can't be that, as Monsieur knows where he is.

M. VANDERK *père.*

So go and see where your father is.

VICTORINE.

Straight away.

SCENE III.

M. VANDERK *père alone.*

In the middle of our most justified happiness... Where is Antoine... I foresaw all human woes awaiting me. I had prepared myself. Even death... But this... What's to be said!... Oh, Heavens!...

SCENE IV.

THE AUNT, M. VANDERK *père.*

M. VANDERK *père, having adopted a calm appearance.*

Well, sister mine, can I at last give myself up to the pleasure of seeing you again?

THE AUNT.

My brother, I'm very angry. You can tell me off later, if you want.

M. VANDERK *père.*

I have every reason to be annoyed with you.

THE AUNT.

As have I with your son.

M. VANDERK *père*.

I thought that in a family there was no need for this sort of manoeuvring, and that a brother...

THE AUNT.

And I thought that a sister like me deserved a certain consideration.

M. VANDERK *père*.

What! Has someone failed you in some way?

THE AUNT.

Yes, certainly.

M. VANDERK *père*.

Who?

THE AUNT.

Your son.

M. VANDERK *père*.

My son! And when can he have offended you?

THE AUNT.

Now.

M. VANDERK *père*.

Now!

THE AUNT.

Yes, Brother, now. It is very peculiar that my nephew, who is supposed to give me his arm today, is not here, and that he has gone out.

M. VANDERK *père*.

He has gone out on essential business.

THE AUNT.

Essential, essential! Your composure amazes me. You must find him for me dead or alive. He is the one who is to give me his arm.

M. VANDERK *père*.

I will give you mine, if necessary.

THE AUNT.

You? Nevertheless, that is fine with me, you will be doing me an honour. Now, Brother, let's have a serious conversation. I've thought of all sorts of things for my nephew, even though it is naughty of him to have gone out. Near to my château, or rather, near to yours, and I'm very grateful to you for it, there is a certain fief that was taken from the family in 1574, but it's not possible to buy it back.

M. VANDERK *père*.

I understand.

THE AUNT.

It's an injustice, but it's also annoying.

M. VANDERK *père*.

That may well be. Let's go and join…

THE AUNT.

We have time. The stained glass in the chapel must be repainted. You're surprised.

M. VANDERK *père*.

We'll talk about it.

THE AUNT.

It's because the coats of arms are quartered with Aragon, and the lambel…[22]

M. VANDERK *père*.

Sister, you are not leaving today.

THE AUNT.

No, certainly not.

M. VANDERK *père*.

Well then, we'll talk about it tomorrow.

---

[22] Quartering is the division of the coat of arms into four parts so that it can incorporate the coats of arms of more than one family. The lambel or label is a horizontal stripe along the top of the coat of arms from which short vertical marks, or pendants, hang.

THE AUNT.

You see, last night I planned for your son, I planned astonishing things. He's adorable, adorable. We have living near us the richest heiress who's a Cramont Ballière de La Tour d'Agon. You know what that means; she's even related to your wife. Your son is going to marry her; I'll sort it out; you won't need to be involved. I'll put him forward, I'll get him married, he'll join the army, and I'll stay with his wife, my niece, and I'll bring up his children.

M. VANDERK *père*.

Oh, Sister!

THE AUNT.

They are your family, Brother.

M. VANDERK *père*.

Let's go into the drawing room; no doubt they will be waiting for us.

SCENE V.

THE ACTORS FROM THE PREVIOUS SCENE, ANTOINE.

M. VANDERK *père to Antoine who enters*.

Antoine, stay here.

THE AUNT *on her way out*.

I see that it's a good thing, a very good thing for my nephew that I've come. You, my brother, have lost all sense of nobility and of greatness. Business diminishes the soul, brother mine. That dear child, that dear child! Oh, I love him with all my heart.

SCENE VI.

ANTOINE *alone*.

Yes, my mind is made up. What? Someone who may be a scoundrel, a rogue…

SCENE VII.

VICTORINE, ANTOINE.

ANTOINE.

What do you want?

VICTORINE.

I was coming in.

ANTOINE.

I don't like all this. Always at my heels. It's quite astonishing. Curiosity, curiosity! Mademoiselle, this is perhaps the last piece of advice I will ever give you, but curiosity in a young woman will certainly make her turn out badly.

VICTORINE.

But I was coming to tell you…

ANTOINE.

Go, go. Listen: be good, and always lead an honest life, and you won't go wrong.

VICTORINE *aside*.

What was that all about?

SCENE VIII.

THE ACTORS FROM THE PREVIOUS SCENE, M. VANDERK *père*.

M. VANDERK *père*.

Go, Victorine. Leave us alone and close the door.

SCENE IX.

M. VANDERK *père*, ANTOINE.

M. VANDERK *père*.

Have you told the surgeon to stay close at hand?

ANTOINE.

No.

M. VANDERK *père*.

No!

ANTOINE.

No, no…

M. VANDERK *père*.

Why not?

ANTOINE.

Why not? Because Monsieur your son won't fight.

M. VANDERK *père*.

What do you mean?

ANTOINE.

Monsieur, Monsieur, a gentleman, a soldier, a devil, even if he were a captain of the king's fleet; it's what they want, but he won't fight, I'm telling you. He can only be an assassin. He picked a quarrel with him. He thinks he's going to kill him, but he won't.

M. VANDERK *père*.

Antoine!

ANTOINE.

No, Monsieur, he won't kill him. I've seen to it… I know which way he'll come; I'll wait for him, I'll attack him, he'll attack me, I'll kill him, or he'll kill me. If he kills me, it will be more of a problem for him than for me. If I kill him, Monsieur, I commend my daughter to you, although I know that I have no need to.

M. VANDERK *père*.

Antoine, what you are suggesting is pointless, and I would never…

ANTOINE.

Your pistols, your pistols. You saw me, you saw me on that ship long ago. What does it matter? As far as valour is concerned, all you need is to be a man, and to be armed.

M. VANDERK *père*.

But Antoine!

ANTOINE.

Monsieur… my dear master, a young man with such prospects. My daughter told me; and today's problems, and the wedding, and all these people, just when… the shop keys. I was taking them with me. (*He gives the keys to M. Vanderk.*) Ah, I'll go mad! Oh gods!

M. VANDERK *père*.

He's breaking my heart. Listen to me; I'm telling you to listen to me.

ANTOINE.

Monsieur.

M. VANDERK *père*.

Do you believe that I don't love my son more than you do?

ANTOINE.

And that's why. It will kill you.

M. VANDERK *père*.

No.

ANTOINE.

Oh, Heavens!

M. VANDERK *père*.

Antoine, you aren't being reasonable! I can't understand you today. Listen to me.

ANTOINE.

Monsieur.

M. VANDERK *père*.

I'm telling you to listen to me. I need you to think clearly. Listen carefully to what I'm going to ask you to do. Someone could come at any moment, and I won't be able to tell you… Do you think, my poor Antoine, do you think, my old friend, that I'm without feelings? Is he not my son? Am I not relying on him for the happiness of my old age? And my wife… Oh, the sorrow of it! Her poor health… But there is no solution; the prejudice that afflicts our nation makes her unhappiness inevitable.

ANTOINE.

Could you not sort out this affair?

M. VANDERK *père*.

Sort it out! You don't know all the complications of the code of honour. Where would we find his opponent? Where would we come across him now? Can things like this be sorted out on the field of honour? Is it not contrary to both custom and the law that I should appear to know about it?... And if my son had hesitated, if he had relented, if this cruel affair had been sorted out, how many more of them would he be preparing for himself in the future! What little man, what man with a modicum of courage, would not feel he could have a go at him. He'd have to have ten victorious encounters to make people forget this one. It's dreadful from every point of view, because he's in the wrong.

ANTOINE.

In the wrong!

M. VANDERK *père*.

It's a stupid mistake.

ANTOINE.

A stupid mistake!

M. VANDERK *père*.

Yes. But let's not waste time on pointless discussions, Antoine.

ANTOINE.

Monsieur.

M. VANDERK *père*.

Do exactly what I'm going to tell you.

ANTOINE.

Yes, Monsieur.

M. VANDERK *père*.

Don't forget any of my instructions; my honour, and the honour of my son depend on it; that should be all I need to say.

ANTOINE.

Heavens!

M. VANDERK *père*.

You are the only one I can confide in, and I trust in your age, your experience, and, I may say, your friendship. Go to the place where they are to meet; disguise yourself so that you cannot be recognized; wait in readiness as far away as you can; if possible, make sure you aren't recognized in any way. If my son has the cruel good fortune to kill his adversary, show yourself then, he'll be upset, he'll be lost, he won't be able to see straight. See for him; give him your full attention; see to his escape; give him your horse, do as he tells you; do what seems sensible to you. Once he's gone, give all possible care to his adversary; if he's still breathing, take charge of his final moments; give him all the help that humanity dictates; atone as far as you can for the crime that I'm participating in, because... because... Cruel honour!... But, Antoine, if Heaven punishes me as much as I deserve, if it takes my son... I'm a father, and I fear what my first reactions will be. I'm a father... and this celebration, this wedding... my wife... her health, me myself. Then you'll hurry here. But because your presence will tell me more than I want to know, do me this favour; listen, do it for me, I beg you. Knock three times on the door of the yard. Three clear knocks, and then come here, in here, in this office. You won't speak to anyone; my horses will be ready; we'll rush there.

ANTOINE.

But, Monsieur...

M. VANDERK *père*.

Someone's coming, and it's his mother.

SCENE X.

THE ACTORS FROM THE PREVIOUS SCENE, MME VANDERK.

MME VANDERK.

My dear, everyone is ready. Here are your gloves. Antoine, oh, look at you! You really should have dressed in black and made yourself smart for the wedding of my daughter. I won't forgive you for that.

ANTOINE.

It's because... Madame... I'm going out on business. Yes, yes... Madame.

M. VANDERK *père*.

Go, go, Antoine. Do what I've told you.

ANTOINE.

Yes, Monsieur.

M. VANDERK *père*.

Don't forget anything.

ANTOINE.

Yes, Monsieur.

MME VANDERK.

Antoine.

ANTOINE.

Madame?

MME VANDERK.

If you come across my son, please tell him to hurry up.

M. VANDERK *père*.

Go, Antoine, go. (*Antoine and M. Vanderk exchange looks; Antoine leaves.*)

SCENE XI.

M. and MME VANDERK.

MME VANDERK.

Antoine seems quite upset.

M. VANDERK *père*.

All of this bothers him and gets him worked up.

MME VANDERK.

Ah, my dear, compliment me; it's more than two years since I felt as well as this… My daughter… my son-in-law, his whole family is so respectable, so honest, good lawyers are as wise as the laws. But, my dear, I have a bone to pick with you, and your sister is right: today of all days you have given a task to your son; you've sent him goodness knows where, and, you know, it must be a long way away, because I'm sure that he hasn't enjoyed it, and when he gets back he won't be able to join us. Victorine has said to my daughter that he wasn't dressed, and that he was on horseback.

M. VANDERK *père, taking her hand affectionately.*

Give me time to get my breath, and, with your permission, I'll think only of making sure you are satisfied. Your good health gives me the greatest pleasure: we need our strength so much; adversity is always so close. The greatest happiness is so uncertain, so... Let's not keep everyone waiting, the company must be missing us. Here they are.

SCENE XII.

THE ACTORS FROM THE PREVIOUS SCENE, SOPHIE, THE SON-IN-LAW, THE AUNT *in the background.*

M. VANDERK *père.*

Come along, you wonderful young people. Madame, we were like that. I hope, my children, that you will see such a day, (*aside*) and better than this one!

End of Act IV.

ACT V.

SCENE I.

VICTORINE *turning back to the entrance she has just come in through.*

Monsieur Antoine, Monsieur Antoine, Monsieur Antoine!.... The maître d'hôtel, the servants, the clerks, everyone is asking for Monsieur Antoine. It's all falling on me. I'm astonished at my father: I've been looking all over for him, and I can't find him anywhere. Never have there been so many people here, and never… Eh?... What now?... Pardon?... Antoine, Antoine. Well, let them call. This ceremony that I thought would be so gay, Heavens, how sad it is… But him! Not to have been at the marriage of his sister, and, on the the other hand, my father too, with his advice: 'Be good, be good, and you won't go wrong…' Where has he gone? I…

SCENE II.

M. DESPARVILLE *père*, VICTORINE.

M. DESPARVILLE *père*.

May I come in, Mademoiselle?

VICTORINE.

You must be with the wedding party, Monsieur. Do go into the drawing room.

M. DESPARVILLE *père*.

No, I'm not, Mademoiselle, I'm not.

VICTORINE.

If you aren't, Monsieur, why are you?...

M. DESPARVILLE *père*.

I'm here to speak to Monsieur Vanderk.

VICTORINE.

Which one?

M. DESPARVILLE *père*.

Well, the merchant. Are there two merchants with that name? It's the one who lives here.

VICTORINE.

Ah, Monsieur, how awkward! I can assure you that I don't know how Monsieur will be able to speak to you in the middle of all of this; they would even be eating, if they weren't waiting for someone who's really keeping them waiting.

M. DESPARVILLE *père*.

Mademoiselle, Monsieur Vanderk has promised to meet with me today at this time.

VICTORINE.

In that case, he didn't know what problems...

M. DESPARVILLE *père*.

He didn't know, he didn't know: it was just yesterday evening that he informed me.

VICTORINE.

I'll go then, if I can get hold of him, as he's in constant demand. I'll say... What should I say?

M. DESPARVILLE *père*.

Tell him it's someone who would like to speak to him; someone he arranged an appointment with for this hour about a letter he received from him... Also tell him that... No... just say that.

VICTORINE.

I'm on my way... Someone!... But, Monsieur, allow me to ask your name.

M. DESPARVILLE *père*.

He doesn't really know it. Still, tell him it's Monsieur Desparville, the master of a servant...

VICTORINE.

Ah, I know him, a man who had a face like... who looked as if... Yesterday evening... I'm going, I'm going.

SCENE III.

M. DESPARVILLE *père alone.*

What a fuss! Good Lord, this is really working out so well for me. This man's daughter had to be getting married precisely today, the day, the very day that I need to speak to him. It's as if it's deliberate. Yes, it's deliberately aimed at me. This sort of thing only happens to me. Damned children! I don't want to get involved in anything more. I'm going to retire to the country. But Father, Father… But Son, leave me alone. I've had my time, get on with yours. Ah, it looks as if this is our man. Yet another refusal that I'm going to endure.

SCENE IV.

M. VANDERK *père*, M. DESPARVILLE *père, an officer awarded the Ordre du Mérite.*

M. DESPARVILLE *père.*

Monsieur, Monsieur, I'm sorry to disturb you. I know all that is happening. Your daughter is getting married, you have guests. But a word, just one word.

M. VANDERK *père.*

And I'm sorry, Monsieur, not to have given you an earlier appointment. Perhaps you've been kept waiting. I said four o'clock, and it's sixteen minutes past three.[23] Sit down, Monsieur.

M. DESPARVILLE *père.*

No, we'll stand; I won't take long. Monsieur, I feel that the devil is after me. I've needed money for a little while, and since yesterday I need it even more for a most urgent turn of events, which I can't tell you about. I have a bill of exchange, which is good, excellent. As your merchants say, it's solid gold. But when will it be paid? I have no idea. They have procedures, delays, terms that I don't understand. I've been to several of your colleagues, usurers, thieves,[24] forgive me for using the word, yes, thieves. They have asked me for high fees, because they can see that I need it. Others have turned me down flat. Can you guess why a man refused me yesterday?

M. VANDERK *père.*

No, Monsieur.

---

[23] In fact, he said 'between three and four' (see act II, scene 5).
[24] The original text uses two traditional racial slurs at this point.

M. DESPARVILLE *père*.

Because this ribbon is blue and not red. Might you possibly think the same?

M. VANDERK *père*.

Monsieur, gentlemen are concerned only with the integrity of their peers, and not with their beliefs.

M. DESPARVILLE *père*.

What you say is just, and the universe would just be one happy family if everyone thought as you do. But I don't want to keep you. Can you advance me the payment of my bill of exchange, or can't you?

M. VANDERK *père*.

May I see it?

M. DESPARVILLE *père*.

Here it is…. (*While M. Vanderk reads it.*) I'll pay whatever is needed. I know there are fees. Do you need a quarter? Do you need… I need money.

M. VANDERK *père*. (*He rings.*)

Monsieur, I'm going to pay it.

M. DESPARVILLE *père*.

Immediately?

M. VANDERK *père*.

Yes, Monsieur.

M. DESPARVILLE *père*.

Immediately! Take it, Monsieur. Oh, what a favour you are doing me! Take it, take it, Monsieur.

(*The servant enters.*)

M. VANDERK *père*.

Go to my cash office, bring me the value of this bill, 2400 livres.

M. DESPARVILLE *père*.

Monsieur, keep the commissioner, the commissionaire, the…

M. VANDERK *père*.

No, Monsieur, I don't take commission, that is not my trade; and I can admit with pleasure that this service costs me nothing. Your bill comes from Cádiz; for me it is a promissory note, which is equivalent to ready cash.

M. DESPARVILLE *père*.

Monsieur, this is indeed honesty, true honesty. You do not know the full extent of the favour you've done me.

M. VANDERK *père*.

I hope it is considerable.

M. DESPARVILLE *père*.

Ah, Monsieur! Monsieur, how happy you are! You have only a daughter?

M. VANDERK *père*.

I hope I have a son.

M. DESPARVILLE *père*.

A son! But I assume he must be in business, in a calm profession. But mine, mine is in the military; as we speak, he is busy fighting.

M. VANDERK *père*.

Fighting!

M. DESPARVILLE *père*.

Yes, Monsieur, fighting; another young man in a café, a little brute picked a quarrel with him; I don't know why; I don't know how; he doesn't know himself.

M. VANDERK *père*.

How I feel for you! How this sort of thing is to be feared!

M. DESPARVILLE *père*.

Feared! I don't fear anything. My son is brave, he takes after me, and skilful, skilful. At twenty paces he could cut a bullet in two by shooting it at the blade of a knife. But he must flee, that's the Hell of it; it's a bad job. You understand, you understand; I am putting my trust in you; I've really taken a liking to you.

M. VANDERK *père*.

Monsieur, I am flattered by your... (*Bang. There is a knock at the door.*) I am flattered that... (*Bang, a second knock.*)

M. DESPARVILLE *père*.

It's nothing, but someone's knocking at your door.

M. VANDERK *père*.

(*Bang, a third knock.*) Ah, Monsieur, not all fathers are unhappy.

M. DESPARVILLE *père*.

Monsieur, are you unwell?

M. VANDERK *père*.

No, Monsieur. (*The servant enters with the 2400 livres.*) Here is your money! Go, Monsieur, you have no time to lose.

M. DESPARVILLE *père*.

Monsieur, I am very much indebted to you! (*He takes a few steps then returns.*) Monsieur, in addition to the favour you are doing me, could I ask you another? Do you have gold? It's because I'm going to give my son...

M. VANDERK *père*.

Yes, Monsieur.

M. DESPARVILLE *père*.

I could lose a huge amount of time in getting together a few louis d'or.

M. VANDERK *père to the servant*.

Take back the two 1200-livre bags. Monsieur, here are four rolls each of twenty-five louis d'or. They are sealed and counted exactly.

M. DESPARVILLE *père*.

Monsieur, I am very much obliged to you.

M. VANDERK *père*.

Go, Monsieur, but forgive me if I don't see you out.

M. DESPARVILLE *père*.

Stay, stay, Monsieur, please. You are busy! What a good man, what an honest man! Monsieur, ask anything of me; stay, stay, stay, please. What an honest man.

SCENE V.

M. VANDERK *père*.

My son is dead... I saw him there... and I didn't embrace him... Oh, Heavens! Why is Antoine taking so long? What pain was in store for me when he was born? What grief his mother!...

SCENE VI.

M. VANDERK *père*, MUSICIANS, *porters carrying cellos and double basses*.

ONE OF THE MUSICIANS.

Is it here, Monsieur?

M. VANDERK *père*.

What do you want? Oh, Heavens! (*He looks at them, trembling, and falls back into his chair.*)

THE MUSICIAN.

We were told to put our instruments here, and we're going to...

SCENE VII.

ANTOINE, THE ACTORS FROM THE PREVIOUS SCENE.

ANTOINE *enters, furious, he grabs them, pushes them, and chases them.*

Go to Hell with your music. Isn't the house big enough?

THE MUSICIAN.

We're going... we're going.

SCENE VIII.

ANTOINE, M. VANDERK *père*.

M. VANDERK *père*.

Well?

ANTOINE.

Oh, Master, both of them. I was a long way off, but I saw, I saw. Oh, Monsieur.

M. VANDERK *père*.

My son.

ANTOINE.

Yes, they galloped towards each other. The officer fired, then your son. First of all the officer fell, he fell first. After that, Monsieur, ah, my dear master, the horses separated, I ran... I...

M. VANDERK *père*.

Go and see if my horses are ready. Bring them to the back entrance, and come and tell me. We must rush there, perhaps he is only wounded.

SCENE IX.

THE ACTORS FROM THE PREVIOUS SCENE, VICTORINE.

ANTOINE.

He's dead, dead. I saw his hat fly off. Dead.

VICTORINE.

Dead. His hat. Whose hat? Dead! Ah, Monsieur!

M. VANDERK *père*.

What do you want?

ANTOINE.

What are you asking? Get out of here immediately.

M. VANDERK *père*.

Leave her. Antoine, go and do what I've told you. What do you want, Victorine?

SCENE X.

M. VANDERK *père*, VICTORINE.

(Antoine is on his way out.)

VICTORINE.

I was coming to ask if the meal should be served, and I met a man who told me that you were unwell.

M. VANDERK *père*.

No, I'm not unwell. Where are the guests?

VICTORINE.

The meal is about to be served.

M. VANDERK *père*.

Try to speak to Madame in private; tell her that I must go out now, and that I don't want her to worry, but that she must behave in such a way that no one notices that I'm not there. Perhaps I'll be… But you are crying, Victorine.

VICTORINE.

Dead. Who then? Monsieur your son?

M. VANDERK *père*.

Victorine.

VICTORINE.

I'm going, Monsieur, I'm going. No, I won't cry, I won't cry.

M. VANDERK *père*.

No, stay. That's an order. Your tears will give you away. I forbid you to leave this room until I get back.

VICTORINE *seeing M. Vanderk fils*.

Ah! Monsieur!

M. VANDERK *père*.

My son!

SCENE XI.

THE ACTORS FROM THE PREVIOUS SCENE, M. VANDERK *fils*, M. DESPARVILLE *père*, M. DESPARVILLE *fils*.

M. VANDERK *fils*.

Father!

M. VANDERK *père*.

Son!… I embrace you… I trust it is an honest man who has returned?

M. DESPARVILLE *père*.

Yes, thank God, it is.

M. VANDERK *fils*.

May I introduce you to Messieurs Desparville.

M. VANDERK *père*.

Messieurs.

M. DESPARVILLE *père*.

Monsieur, may I introduce you to my son. Was it not my son, was it not precisely him who was his opponent?

M. VANDERK *père*.

How is it possible that this business…

M. DESPARVILLE *père*.

All is well, well, Heavens it is well! I'll tell you what happened.

M. DESPARVILLE *fils*.

Father, let me speak.

M. VANDERK *fils*.

What are you going to say?

M. DESPARVILLE *fils*.

Let me get my own back.

M. VANDERK *fils*.

Get your own back, then.

M. DESPARVILLE *fils*.

The story would be too brief if you told it, Monsieur, and at present I share your happiness. (*To M. Vanderk père.*) I have the impression, Monsieur, that you were as well informed as my father. But this is what you don't know. We met; I raced up to him; I fired; he tore towards me; he said: 'I'm firing into the air', and he did. 'Listen', he said, riding towards me, 'I thought yesterday that you were insulting my father when you spoke of merchants. I insulted you. I've realized I was wrong; I'm apologizing to you. If you aren't content, ride off, and we'll start over again.' Monsieur, I can't explain what I felt. I threw myself from my horse, he did the same, and we embraced. I met my father, my father who, during all of this, you were helping. Oh, Monsieur!

M. DESPARVILLE *père*.

And, good Lord, you knew, and I wager that those three knocks at the door… What a man you are! And during that time you were helping me! I am strong, I'm honest, but at a time like that, in your place, I would have told the Baron Desparville to go to the devil.

M. VANDERK *père*.

Ah, Messieurs, how difficult it is to pass from great grief to great joy!

VICTORINE *seizes the son's hat.*

Heavens, Monsieur!

M. VANDERK *fils*.

What is it, Victorine?

VICTORINE.

There's a bullet hole in your hat!

M. DESPARVILLE *fils*.

A bullet hole! Ah, my friend! (*They embrace.*)

M. VANDERK *père*.

Messieurs, I can hear noises. We are sitting down to eat; do me the honour of joining us for the wedding dinner. None of this must get out, it would spoil the celebration. After what has happened, Monsieur, you can be only the greatest enemy or the greatest friend of my son, and we're not giving you a choice.

M. DESPARVILLE *fils kisses the hand of M. Vanderk père.*

Ah, Monsieur!

M. DESPARVILLE *père*.

Good, good, my son. That is well done.

VICTORINE.

'Only to me, only to me', how cruel.

M. VANDERK *fils*.

How pleased I am to see you again, my dear Victorine.

M. VANDERK *père*.

Victorine, leave us.

SCENE XII.

MME VANDERK, SOPHIE, THE SON-IN-LAW, and THE ACTORS FROM THE PREVIOUS SCENE.

MME VANDERK.

Ah, there you are, Son. (*To M. Vanderk père.*) My dear, can we have the meal served? It's late.

M. VANDERK *père*.

These gentlemen would like to stay. Let me introduce my wife, my son-in-law, and my daughter to you, Messieurs.

M. DESPARVILLE *père*.

Such a family deserves great happiness.

SCENE XIII.

THE AUNT, and THE ACTORS FROM THE PREVIOUS SCENE.

THE AUNT.

I'm told that my nephew has arrived. Ah, there you are, my dear child.

M. VANDERK *père*.

Madame, you wanted military men, here they are. Help me persuade them to stay.

THE AUNT.

Oh, it's old Baron Desparville.

M. DESPARVILLE *père*.

And it's you, Madame la Marquise. I thought you were in Berry.

THE AUNT.

What are you doing here?

M. DESPARVILLE *père*.

Madame, you are at the home of the most considerate man, the most, the most…

M. VANDERK *père*.

Monsieur, Monsieur, let us go into the drawing room and you can renew your acquaintance. Messieurs, my children, I am overcome by the greatest joy. Madame, here is our son.

(*He embraces him, the son embraces his mother.*)

SCENE XIV.

ANTOINE and THE ACTORS FROM THE PREVIOUS SCENE.

ANTOINE.

The carriage is ready, Monsieur, and… Oh, Heavens! Good gods! Oh, Monsieur!

MME VANDERK.

All right, all right, Antoine! But his head's spinning today.

THE AUNT.

This man is quite mad.

(*Victorine rushes over to her father, puts her hand over his mouth, and hugs him.*)

M. VANDERK *père*.

Quiet, Antoine. See to having the meal served.

ANTOINE.

I don't know if it's a dream. What happiness! I must have been blind… Ah, youngsters, youngsters, will you never realize that even the most excusable folly can cause grief to all around you?

End of Act V.

APPENDIX OF REVISED SCENES

The text presented in Sedaine's supplement is arranged in four blocks. The first and shortest of these begins part way through act II, scene 5 with the servant's reply to Vanderk *père*'s question 'Served?' and goes on to the end of that scene. The reference in the original version to the fact that Desparville *père* is a Protestant is cut in the revision. The only other modification is an addition to the servant's exit line presumably intended as a reminder to the audience of the reason Vanderk *père* is preoccupied.

The second block begins part way through act III, scene 8 with Vanderk *fils*'s line 'If it were possible that I might insist on one thing from you…', and continues to the end of the act. In scene 8, lines stressing the fact that honour dictates that Vanderk *fils* must fight are suppressed, as is the detail that the participants will fight with pistols, not swords, but the revised version, clearly to please the censors, also elaborates on the reasons for Vanderk *père*'s statement that laws against duelling are just. The writing of letters by Vanderk *père* to aid his son's escape is removed from scene 9. In the original text Vanderk *fils* returned in scene 11 both to bring his father the letter he had written to him, and to collect the letters the father has written to aid his escape. Since both the writing of the letters by Vanderk *père* in scene 9 and his explanation to his son of how to make use of them found in the original scene 11 have been removed to satisfy the censors, there is no need for Vanderk *fils* to return, so the scene is cut, with details about the time and location of the duel that need to be preserved being moved to scene 8; an explanation of what should be done with Vanderk *fils*'s letter to his father is added to the end of scene 10. In the original scene 12, now renumbered 11, a comment that the laws against duelling are inadequate is removed, and the revised scene 13, now 12, contains the detail that Vanderk *fils* has taken his pistols with him, presumably because the fact that the duel was to be fought with pistols has been removed from scene 8; it is true that the pistols have already been mentioned in act III, scene 2, but since that comes before the scenes concerning the duel, their full significance would not necessarily have been obvious, hence the need for this reminder here.

The third block begins at the beginning of act V, scene 4, and, in that scene, another reference to Desparville *père*'s Protestantism is removed. The other main difference here, one that Sedaine attributes to audience reaction rather than censorship, is that Desparville *père*'s request that he be paid in gold and Vanderk *père*'s ready agreement to the request are moved to well before the three knocks rather than just after them. Presumably Vanderk *père*'s stoicism in helping the father of the man he now believes to be his son's killer was thought by audiences to be too far-fetched. The extract continues into scene 5, where the only modification to the original is the removal of a line suggesting that Antoine is taking a long time. The next two short scenes, 6 and 7, which provided the comic relief of the arrival of the musicians, who are subsequently chased by Antoine, were both cut as part of the revision. The introduction of a comic incident at this point was clearly too much for an audience used to the French classical ban on the mixing of comedy and tragedy. The block continues with the original scenes 8 and 9, now renumbered 6 and 7, but there are no significant changes in either. The text of this block ends here, hence scene 10 and the beginning of scene 11 from the original, now renumbered 8 and 9, are unchanged.

Block four begins part way through the original act V, scene 11, scene 9 in the revised version, beginning at Vanderk *père*'s line 'Ah, Messieurs, how difficult it is to pass from great grief to great joy!', and continues until the end of the play. This block perhaps most typifies the fact that Sedaine clearly wished his audience to appreciate the variations in the original text in context, for, after the exchange between Victorine and Vanderk *fils* about the fact that there is a bullet hole in his hat, which comes soon after the beginning of the extract and which is cut in the revised version, he continues with three more scenes right to the end of the play despite the fact that there are only two other minor modifications, neither of which would appear to have anything to do with the censors: the addition in the revision of some complaints for the Aunt at the beginning of the penultimate scene, and of her assertion that Antoine should be locked up in the final scene.

As mentioned in the introduction, this appendix does not contain the scenes originally included in Sedaine's own supplement, the scenes from his original text that were modified because of censorship or adverse audience reaction. These have been restored to the main text, so included here are the revised versions of those scenes that replaced them in performance and were included in the main text of the original editions.

Sedaine's introduction, found at the beginning of the supplement, follows:

Of all my play's faults, the one that does not escape even the most superficial scrutiny is that it does not fulfil its title; I have been the first to say so after the changes. My *Philosophe sans le savoir* was a man of honour, who sees all the cruelty of a terrible prejudice, and who is pained to give in to it. Looking at it in a different way, it is Brutus, who, inspired by what he owes to his country, stifles the voice of reason, the cry of nature, and sends his sons to their deaths.[1]

---

[1] Lucius Junius Brutus, not to be confused with the assassin of Julius Caesar, Marcus Junius Brutus, is said in the sixth century BCE to have overthrown his uncle, the king of Rome Tarquinius Superbus, to found the Roman Empire and become one of the first consuls. When his two sons were among the participants in a plot to restore the monarchy, they were condemned to death along with the other conspirators. Brutus's stoicism in watching their execution made him a famous figure in literature and art in the eighteenth century.

The wisest considerations forced me to change that situation, and to weaken my principal character. I admit that the title of *Philosophe* seemed to present Vanderk as a model in his conduct, and that so-called model, unfortunately too close to our customs, was too far from our laws. But if this work has the good fortune to be performed abroad, national considerations no longer applying, because the setting is not the same for them, I believe that the character of my *Philosophe* as he was will have more motivation, and he will be more effective on the stage; the changes from firmness to affection will have more force, and will become more theatrical.

This is why I have decided to add to the play as it is performed, the scenes as they were before being changed, and I have even restored what the public forced me to cut: the giving of the gold after the knocks, the arrival of the musicians, etc. It is not that the public was not perceptive and did not make good decisions. I had reduced the force, the spirit, and the strength of my athlete, and I had left him with the same weight to carry; the proportions were no longer right. I want performances, wherever they take place, to confirm my thinking to be correct.

ACT II.

From SCENE V.

THE SERVANT.

Yes, he was an officer… a respected officer even…

M. VANDERK *père*.

Tell your master, tell M. Desparville, that I'll be here at his service tomorrow between three and four in the afternoon.

THE SERVANT.

I will.

M. VANDERK *père*.

And please tell him that I am very sorry not to be able to give him an earlier appointment; I am very tied up.

THE SERVANT.

Oh, I know, I know… The wedding of Mademoiselle your daughter… I know, I know.

(*He turns in the direction of the shop.*)

ANTOINE.

Hey, where are you going? To go back to sleep!

* *
*

ACT III.

From SCENE VIII.

M. VANDERK *fils*.

If it were possible that I might insist on one thing from you… Promise me that, whatever I have to tell you, your kindness won't stop me doing what I must do.

M. VANDERK *père*.

If it's just.

M. VANDERK *fils*.

Just or not.

M. VANDERK *père*.

Just or not?

M. VANDERK *fils*.

Don't be alarmed. Yesterday evening I had an argument, a dispute with a cavalry officer. We went outside. We were separated… We have given our word to meet today.

M. VANDERK *père, supporting himself on the back of a chair.*

Oh, my son!

M. VANDERK *fils*.

Father, this is what I was afraid of.

M. VANDERK *père*.

And will you tell me about your quarrel in more detail and what caused it; in fact, everything that happened?

M. VANDERK *fils*.

Ah, I've done everything I could to avoid seeing you.

M. VANDERK *père*.

Does it upset you?

M. VANDERK *fils*.

Never, never have I needed a friend so much, you in particular.

M. VANDERK *père*.

So you had an argument.

M. VANDERK *fils*.

It's not a long story. The rain we had yesterday forced me to go into a café. I was playing a game of chess. I heard someone quite close to me talking heatedly. He was telling some story or other about his father, about a merchant, and fees charged on promissory notes. But I'm certain that I heard quite distinctly: 'Yes… all these merchants, all these businessmen are rogues and scoundrels.' I turned round and looked at him. Without any attention or regard for who might hear him, he repeated what he'd just said. I got up; I said in his ear that only a dishonest man could make such comments. We went outside. We were separated.

M. VANDERK *père*.

Will you allow me to say…

M. VANDERK *fils*.

Oh, Father, I know all the objections you can make. The officer might have been having a moment of bad temper; what he was saying might have had nothing to do with me; when you say everybody, you don't mean anybody; it's even possible he was only repeating what someone else had said to him. And this is why I'm tormented with grief. I've been tortured by my soul-searching. I must try to kill someone who may not be in the wrong. Still, I believe he said it, because I was there.

M. VANDERK *père*.

That's what you want to believe. Does he know you?

M. VANDERK *fils*.

I don't know him.

M. VANDERK *père*.

And you have sought a quarrel? Oh, Son, why did you not think that you had your father? I so often think that I have a son.

M. VANDERK *fils.*

It's because I thought that.

M. VANDERK *père.*

And into what uncertainty, what pain were you going to throw me and your mother today!

M. VANDERK *fils.*

I'd seen to that.

M. VANDERK *père.*

How?

M. VANDERK *fils.*

I'd left on my table a letter addressed to you. Victorine would have given it to you.

M. VANDERK *père.*

Did you confide in Victorine?

M. VANDERK *fils.*

No, but she had to put something back on my table, and she would have seen it.

M. VANDERK *père.*

And what precautions have you taken against the legitimate force of the law?

M. VANDERK *fils.*

The legitimate force of the law!

M. VANDERK *père.*

Yes, these laws are legitimate... One nation... I'm not sure which one... The Romans, I think, rewarded anyone who saved the life of a citizen. What punishment might a Frenchman deserve when he considers killing another Frenchman, when he plans a murder!

M. VANDERK *fils.*

A murder!

M. VANDERK *père.*

Yes, Son, a murder. The confidence that the aggressor has in his own strength is almost always the source of his recklessness.

M. VANDERK *fils*.

And what about you, Father, when on that occasion in the past…

M. VANDERK *père*.

Heaven is just. It is punishing me for that through you. So, what precautions have you taken against the legitimate force of the law?

M. VANDERK *fils*.

To go on the run.

M. VANDERK *père*.

So, what were your plans? The place, the time?

M. VANDERK *fils*.

Three in the afternoon, behind the low ramparts.

M. VANDERK *père*.

Why, then, were you going out so early?

M. VANDERK *fils*.

So that I didn't break my word. I was afraid of the fuss of this wedding, of my aunt, and of finding myself tied up so that I couldn't escape. How I wish it could have been a day later.

M. VANDERK *père*.

And couldn't you stay here from now to three o'clock?

M. VANDERK *fils*.

Father! Just think…

M. VANDERK *père*.

You had your reason, but that reason no longer exists. Have your horses put back and go up to your apartment. I'm going to think of ways of saving both your honour and your life.

M. VANDERK *fils*.

(*Aside.*) To save my honour!… Father, in my misfortune I deserve you to feel sorry for me more than angry.

M. VANDERK *père*.

I'm not angry.

M. VANDERK *fils*.

Prove it to me, then, by letting me embrace you.

M. VANDERK *père*.

No, Monsieur, go back up to your apartment.

M. VANDERK *fils*.

I'm on my way, Father.

(*He leaves quickly.*)

SCENE IX.

M. VANDERK *père alone*.

What a misfortune! How fragile our present happiness is. I went to bed the most peaceful and happiest of fathers, and look at me now! Antoine… I can't be too confident… If he were to shed his blood for his king and country!… But…

SCENE X.

ANTOINE, M. VANDERK *père*.

ANTOINE.

What is it you want?

M. VANDERK *père*.

What I want? That he lives!

ANTOINE.

Monsieur?

M. VANDERK *père*.

I didn't hear you come in.

ANTOINE.

You called me.

M. VANDERK *père*.

I called you?… Antoine, I know your discretion, your friendship for me and for my son. He was going out to fight.

ANTOINE.

Who with? I'll go and…

M. VANDERK *père*.

There's no point.

ANTOINE.

Everyone in the area will defend him. I'll go and wake up…

M. VANDERK *père*.

No, that's not what…

ANTOINE.

You'll have to kill me rather than…

M. VANDERK *père*.

Quiet, he's here. Hurry to his apartment. Tell him, tell him that I want him to send me the letter that he has just been telling me about. Don't say anything else. Don't show any interest in him… Mind you… Go. He must give you that letter and wait for me. I'll go and see him.

SCENE XI.

Omitted.

SCENE XII renumbered XI.

M. VANDERK *père alone.*

Oh Heavens! To trample on reason, nature, and the law. What a fatal prejudice! This cruel abuse of the point of honour could only have been born in the most barbaric era. It could survive only in the midst of a nation that is vain and full of itself, amidst a people in which each individual thinks he is everything, and his country and family nothing. And you, wise laws, you wanted to put a curb on honour; you have ennobled the scaffold; your severity has meant that the heart of a decent man is torn between disgrace and execution. Oh, my son!

Appendix of Revised Scenes

SCENE XIII renumbered XII.

ANTOINE, M. VANDERK *père*.

ANTOINE.

Monsieur, have you let him go?

M. VANDERK *père*.

He's gone! O Heavens! Stop…

ANTOINE.

Ah, Monsieur, he has already gone a long way. I was crossing the courtyard; he has attached his pistols to his saddle.

M. VANDERK *père*.

His pistols!

ANTOINE.

He shouted to me, 'Antoine, look after my father', and he galloped off.

M. VANDERK *père*.

He's gone! Oh Heavens! (*He is lost in deep thought, then he regains his strength, and says:*) No one here must know about this. Come with me. I'm going to get dressed.

End of Act III.

* * *

ACT V.

SCENE IV.

M. VANDERK *père*, M. DESPARVILLE *père*, A SERVANT.

M. DESPARVILLE *père*.

Monsieur, Monsieur, I'm sorry to disturb you. I know all that is happening. Your daughter is getting married today. You have guests. But a word, just one word.

Appendix of Revised Scenes

M. VANDERK *père*.

And I'm sorry, Monsieur, not to have given you an earlier appointment. Perhaps you've been kept waiting. I said four o'clock, and it's sixteen minutes past three.[2] Sit down, Monsieur.

M. DESPARVILLE *père*.

No, we'll stand; I won't take long. Monsieur, I feel that the devil is after me. I've needed money for a few days, and need it even more since yesterday for a most urgent turn of events, which I can't tell you about… I have a bill of exchange, which is good, excellent. As your merchants say, it's solid gold. But when will it be paid? When? I have no idea. They have procedures, delays, terms that I don't understand. I've been to several of your colleagues, but all those I've seen up to now are thieves, usurers;[3] forgive me for using the word, yes, usurers. Some have asked me for high fees, because they can see that I need it. Others have turned me down flat. But I don't want to keep you. Can you advance me the payment of my bill of exchange, or can't you?

M. VANDERK *père*.

May I see it?

M. DESPARVILLE *père*.

Here it is…. (*While M. Vanderk reads it.*) I'll pay whatever is needed. I know there are fees. Do you need a quarter? Do you need… I need money.

M. VANDERK *père*. (*He rings; the bell can be heard.*)

Monsieur, I'm going to pay it.

M. DESPARVILLE *père*.

Immediately?

M. VANDERK *père*.

Yes, Monsieur.

M. DESPARVILLE *père*.

Immediately! Take it, take it, Monsieur. Oh, what a favour you are doing me! Take it, take it, Monsieur.

---

[2] As in the original, he actually said 'between three and four' (see the revised act II, scene 5).
[3] As in the original, the revised text uses two traditional racial slurs at this point.

M. VANDERK *père to the servant he rang for.*

Go to my cash office, bring me the value of this bill, 2400 livres.

M. DESPARVILLE *père.*

Monsieur, in addition to the favour you are doing me, could I ask you another, to give me the sum in gold?

M. VANDERK *père.*

Certainly, Monsieur. (*To the servant.*) Bring the amount in gold.

M. DESPARVILLE *père to the servant who is leaving.*

Monsieur, keep the commission, the fee.

M. VANDERK *père.*

No, Monsieur, I don't take commission, that is not my trade. And I can admit with pleasure that this service costs me nothing. Your bill comes from Cádiz; for me it is a promissory note, which is equivalent to ready cash.

M. DESPARVILLE *père.*

Monsieur, Monsieur, this is indeed honesty, true honesty. You do not know how much I am obliged to you, the full extent of the favour you've done me.

M. VANDERK *père.*

I hope it is considerable.

M. DESPARVILLE *père.*

Ah, Monsieur! Monsieur, how happy you are! You have only a daughter?

M. VANDERK *père.*

I hope I have a son.

M. DESPARVILLE *père.*

A son! But I assume he must be in business, in a calm profession. But mine, mine is in the miltary; as we speak, he is busy fighting.

M. VANDERK *père.*

Fighting!

M. DESPARVILLE *père.*

Yes, Monsieur, fighting, another young man in a café. A little fool picked a quarrel with him; I don't know why; I don't know how; he doesn't know himself.

M. VANDERK *père*.

How I feel for you! How this sort of thing is to be feared!

M. DESPARVILLE *père*.

Feared! I don't fear anything. My son is brave, he takes after me, and skilful, skilful. At twenty paces he could cut a bullet in two by shooting it at the blade of a knife. But he must flee, that's the Hell of it. You understand, you understand; I am putting my trust in you; I've really taken a liking to you.

M. VANDERK *père*.

Monsieur, I am flattered by your… (*There is a knock at the door.*) I am flattered that… (*A second knock.*)

M. DESPARVILLE *père*.

It's nothing, but someone's knocking at your door. (*A third knock.*)

(*M. Vanderk falls onto a chair.*)

M. DESPARVILLE *père*.

Monsieur, are you unwell?

M. VANDERK *père*.

Ah, Monsieur, not all fathers are unhappy. (*The servant enters with rolls of louis d'or.*) Here is your money. Go, Monsieur, you have no time to lose.

M. DESPARVILLE *père*.

I am very much indebted to you.

M. VANDERK *père*.

Forgive me if I don't see you out.

M. DESPARVILLE *père*.

Of course, you are busy! What a good man, what an honest man! Monsieur, ask anything of me; stay, stay, stay, please.

SCENE V.

M. VANDERK *père alone*.

My son is dead… I saw him there… and I didn't embrace him!… Oh Heavens!… What pain was in store for me when he was born? What grief his mother!…

SCENE VI.

Omitted.

SCENE VII.

Omitted.

SCENE VIII renumbered VI.

M. VANDERK *père*, ANTOINE.

M. VANDERK *père*.

Well?

ANTOINE.

Oh, Master, both of them. I was a long way off, but I saw, I saw… Oh, Monsieur!

M. VANDERK *père*.

My son!

ANTOINE.

Yes, they galloped towards each other. The officer fired, then your son. First of all the officer fell, he fell first. After that, Monsieur, ah, my dear master! The horses separated… I ran… I… I…

M. VANDERK *père*.

Go and see if my horses are ready. Bring them to the back entrance, and come and tell me. We must rush there, perhaps he is only wounded.

ANTOINE.

He's dead, dead. I saw his hat fly off. Dead.

SCENE IX renumbered VII.

THE ACTORS FROM THE PREVIOUS SCENE, VICTORINE.

VICTORINE.

Dead! Ah, who? Who?

M. VANDERK *père*.

What do you want?

ANTOINE.

What are you asking? Get out of here immediately.

M. VANDERK *père*.

Leave her. Antoine, go and do what I've told you.

*
* *

From SCENE XI renumbered IX.

MM. VANDERK *père* and *fils*, MM. DESPARVILLE *père* and *fils*, VICTORINE.

M. VANDERK *père*.

Ah, Messieurs, how difficult it is to pass from great grief to great joy! Messieurs, I can hear noises. We were sitting down to eat; do me the honour of joining us for the wedding dinner. None of this must get out, it would spoil the celebration. (*To M. Desparville fils.*) After what has happened, Monsieur, you can be only the greatest enemy or the greatest friend of my son, and we're not giving you a choice.

M. DESPARVILLE *fils*.

Ah, Monsieur! (*Kissing the hand of M. Vanderk père.*)

M. DESPARVILLE *père to his son*.

My son, that is well done.

VICTORINE *to M. Vanderk fils*.

'Only to me, only to me', how cruel.

M. VANDERK *fils to Victorine*.

How pleased I am to see you again.

M. VANDERK *père*.

Victorine, be quiet.

SCENE XII renumbered X.

THE ACTORS FROM THE PREVIOUS SCENE, MME VANDERK, SOPHIE, THE SON-IN-LAW.

MME VANDERK.

Ah, there you are, Son. (*To M. Vanderk père.*) My dear, can we have the meal served? It's late.

M. VANDERK *père*.

These gentlemen would like to stay. (*To the Desparvilles.*) Let me introduce my wife, my son-in-law, and my daughter to you, Messieurs.

M. DESPARVILLE *père*.

Such a family deserves great happiness.

SCENE XIII renumbered XI.

THE ACTORS FROM THE PREVIOUS SCENE, THE AUNT.

THE AUNT.

I'm told that my nephew has arrived. Ah, there you are, my dear child. I couldn't wait to see you. I've asked after you, I've wanted to see you. Your father is strange, very strange to give you an errand on the day of your sister's wedding!

M. VANDERK *père*.

Madame, you wanted military men, here they are. Help me persuade them to stay.

THE AUNT.

Oh, it's old Baron Desparville.

M. DESPARVILLE *père*.

And it's you, Madame la Marquise. I thought you were in Berry.

THE AUNT.

What are you doing here?

M. DESPARVILLE *père*.

Madame, you are at the home of the most considerate man, the most, the most...

M. VANDERK *père*.

Monsieur, Monsieur, let us go into the drawing room and you can renew your acquaintance. Messieurs, my children, I am overcome by the greatest joy. (*To his wife.*) Madame, here is our son.

(He embraces his son, the son embraces his mother.)

SCENE XIV renumbered XII.

THE ACTORS FROM THE PREVIOUS SCENE, ANTOINE.

ANTOINE.

The carriage is ready, Monsieur, and... Oh, Heavens!... Good gods!... Oh, Monsieur!

MME VANDERK.

All right, all right, Antoine! But his head's spinning today.

THE AUNT.

This man is quite mad; he should be locked up.

VICTORINE.

(She rushes over to her father, puts her hand over his mouth, and hugs him.)

M. VANDERK *père*.

Quiet, Antoine. See to having the meal served.

(The company leaves, but Antoine says:)

ANTOINE.

I don't know if it's a dream. What happiness! I must have been blind... Ah, youngsters, youngsters, will you never realize that even the most excusable folly can cause grief to all around you?

End of Act V.

BIBLIOGRAPHY

CHARLTON, DAVID and MARK LEDBURY, eds, *Michel-Jean Sedaine (1719–1797): Theatre, Opera and Art* (Aldershot: Ashgate, 2000)
CONNON, DEREK, *Innovation and Renewal: A Study of the Theatrical Works of Diderot*, Studies on Voltaire and the Eighteenth Century, 258 (Oxford: The Voltaire Foundation, 1989)
DIDEROT, DENIS, *Entretiens sur 'Le Fils naturel'*, in Diderot, *Œuvres esthétiques*, ed. by Paul Vernière (Paris: Garnier, 1968), pp. 69–175
—— *Est-il bon? Est-il méchant?*, ed. by Pierre Frantz ([Paris]: Gallimard, 2012)
—— *Paradoxe sur le comédien*, in Diderot, *Œuvres esthétiques*, ed. by Paul Vernière (Paris: Garnier, 1968), pp. 298–381
FREUD, HILDE H., *Palissot and 'Les Philosophes'*, Diderot Studies, 9 (Geneva: Droz, 1967)
GAIFFE, FÉLIX, *Le Drame en France au XVIIIe siècle* (Paris: Armand Colin, 1910)
GAY, PETER, *The Enlightenment: An Interpretation*, 2 vols (New York: Knopf, 1966–69)
GRIMM, FRIEDRICH MELCHIOR, *Correspondance littéraire, philosophique et critique*, ed. by Maurice Tourneux, 16 vols (Paris: Garnier, 1877–82)
LEDBURY, MARK, *Sedaine, Greuze and the Boundaries of Genre*, Studies on Voltaire and the Eighteenth Century, 380 (Oxford: The Voltaire Foundation, 2000)
LOUGH, JOHN, *Paris Theatre Audiences in the Seventeenth and Eighteenth Centuries* (London: Oxford University Press, 1957)
MASON, H. T., 'Commerce, Class-distinction and Realist Drama: Sedaine (1719–97)', in H. T. Mason, *French Writers and their Society 1715–1800* (London: Palgrave Macmillan, 1982), pp. 146–67
—— '*Le Philosophe sans le savoir*: An Aristocratic *Drame Bourgeois*?', *French Studies*, 30 (1976), 405–18
MAZA, SARAH, *The Myth of the French Bourgeoisie: An Essay on the Social Imaginary, 1750–1850* (Cambridge, MA: Harvard University Press, 2003)
PALISSOT, CHARLES, *Les Philosophes*, in *Théâtre du XVIIIe siècle*, ed. by Jacques Truchet, 2 vols ([Paris]: Gallimard, 1972–74), II, 143–204, 1383–95
—— *The Philosophes*, trans. by Jessica Goodman and others, ed. by Jessica Goodman and Olivier Ferret (Cambridge: Open Book Publishers, 2021)
Registres de la Comédie-Française <https://ui.cfregisters.org/plays>
SAND, GEORGE, *Le Mariage de Victorine, pour faire suite au 'Philosophe sans le savoir' de Sedaine* (Brussels: Lelong, 1851)
SEDAINE, MICHEL-JEAN, *Den virkelig Viise, et Skuespil i 5 Akter, oversat efter Sedaines 'le Philosoph [sic] sans le savoir'*, ved Friderich [ie Frederik] Schwarz (Copenhagen: n. pub., 1787)
—— *Der Philosoph ohne es zu wissen, ein Lustspiel aus dem Französischen des Herrn Sedaine, für ein Privat-Theater übersetzt* (Dresden: Walther, 1776)

—— *Der Philosoph ohne es zu wissen, ein Schauspiel in fünf Aufzügen, aus dem Französischen des Herrn Sedaine übersetzt* (Frankfurt: Johann Gottlieb Garbe, 1767)

—— *Discours prononcés dans l'Académie Françoise, le jeudi XXVII avril M. DCC. LXXXVI, à la réception de M. Sedaine* (Paris: Demonville, 1786)

—— *Il Filosofo senza saper d'esserlo, dramma del Signor Sedaine, traduzione inedita del Signor abate Placido Bordoni* (Venice: Antonio Rosa, 1805)

—— *Le Philosophe sans le savoir* (Paris: Hérissant, 1766)

—— *Le Philosophe sans le savoir*, 2nd edn (Paris: Hérissant, 1766)

—— *Le Philosophe sans le savoir*, ed. by John Dunkley (Egham: Runnymede Books, 1993)

—— *Le Philosophe sans le savoir*, ed. by Graham E. Rodmell (Durham: University of Durham Press, 1987)

—— *Le Philosophe sans le savoir*, ed. by Jacques Truchet, in *Théâtre du XVIIIe siècle*, 2 vols ([Paris]: Gallimard, 1972–74), II, 517–64, 1445–56

—— *Michel-Jean Sedaine, Théâtre de la Révolution*, ed. by Mark Darlow, Critical Texts, 63 (Cambridge, Modern Humanities Research Association, 2017)

—— 'Quelques réflexions inédites de Sedaine sur l'opéra comique', in René-Charles Guilbert de Pixerécourt, *Théâtre choisi*, IV (Paris: Tresse; Nancy: Chez l'Auteur, 1843), 501–16

—— *The Duel, a Play, as Performed at the Theatre-Royal in Drury-Lane*, trans. by William O'Brien (London: Davies, 1772)

Théâtre du XVIIIe siècle, ed. by Jacques Truchet, 2 vols ([Paris]: Gallimard, 1972–74)

WADE, IRA OWEN, 'The Title of Sedaine's *Le Philosophe sans le savoir*', *PMLA*, 43 (1928), 1026–38

www.ingramcontent.com/pod-product-compliance
Lightning Source LLC
Chambersburg PA
CBHW071512150426
43191CB00009B/1499